D0379871

CREATIVE
CURE

THE
CREATIVE
CURE

HOW FINDING AND FREEING YOUR
INNER ARTIST CAN HEAL YOUR LIFE

Jacob Nordby

Hierophantpublishing

Cover design by Emma Smith
Cover art by Luis Portugal | iStock
Print book interior design by Frame25 Productions

Hierophant Publishing
8301 Broadway, Suite 219
San Antonio, TX 78209
www.hierophantpublishing.com

If you are unable to order this book from your local bookseller,
you may order directly from the publisher.

Library of Congress Control Number: 2020949053

ISBN: 978-1-950253-04-3

10 9 8 7 6 5 4 3 2 1

For Brie, who helped me write this book
in many more ways than you know.

Applying creativity to healing changed everything.
I believe that creativity in motion heals everything.

—SARK

Contents

Foreword

I want you to be able to picture the author who is, for me, a cherished friend. I met Jacob Nordby teaching together in Santa Fe, and he gave me a copy of a book he'd written. I looked at the cover, which was both bold and brash, and said to myself, "It's not for me." Nonetheless, I took the book home and put it on a side table, where, for several months, it confronted me. One lonely night—I live alone with a small dog—I picked up the book and began reading. To my surprise and delight, the book was wonderful. On impulse, I grabbed the phone, dialing Nordby's number. When he answered, I introduced myself—"This is Julia Cameron, and I think you are an absolutely wonderful writer." Taken aback, Nordby managed to say, "Really? I mean, thank you!" And thus, a friendship was struck.

Barrel-chested, bearded, and twinkly eyed, Nordby didn't conform to any image of the suffering artist. His prose was magical, spirited, sensual, and spiritual. For me, an intoxicating mixture. Grounded as I am in a four-decades-plus spiritual path, I found Nordby's writing to be both accurate and invigorating. He was indeed, as one of his titles suggested, a divine arsonist—lighting the fire of spiritual hunger in his reader.

When I was asked to write the foreword for this current book, I happily agreed. I had come to know Nordby over several years' friendship to be a lively and engaging teacher. The authenticity of his message was beyond the shadow of a doubt. A spiritual practitioner himself, he led others forward into their own deepening spirituality. Like me, he saw spirituality and creativity to be inextricably linked.

A veteran teacher, blending his love of words with his love of God, he forged something called, "the creative cure." Using tools he had tried, tested, and applied, he sought to open what he called, "our inner creative nature." As he wrote, "for me, spirituality and creativity describe the same thing: the way we celebrate the timeless, essential energy of life." Sensitive to the reservations of his readers, he added, "furthermore, since creativity as a spiritual practice doesn't dictate any particular beliefs or traditions, it can work in harmony with any other religious or spiritual customs you may also enjoy."

In other words, be open-minded. No matter what your convictions, Nordby's tools can resonate for you. I want to say, read this book slowly. Or perhaps, read it twice. The tasks and playful exercises are challenging. Nordby believes "in the play of ideas," and play is an essential part of his message. While writing of serious matters—socialization, trauma, and rejection—he writes with an engaged intelligence and a veterans' confidence that creative wounds can be healed and even cured. The "creative cure" is one that Nordby has both witnessed and instigated in his teaching. Throughout the book he shares personal stories that anchor his intellectual ideas firmly in daily life.

I think this book serves as an entryway into deep creative waters—waters that the reader may find both bracing and invigorating. I share with Nordby a love of tools that "work," and I found myself drawn to the simplicity and subtlety of the methods he suggests for unlocking a powerful and joyous self that we may have buried or forgotten. I know from our friendship that Nordby practices what he preaches—a lively mix of journaling, meditation, and guidance. It is my wish that the reader encounter in these pages both the man and the muse, catalyzing a creative cure that infiltrates all arenas of life.

—Julia Cameron, author of *The Artist's Way*

Introduction

If a child comes to you with a wound, say a badly skinned knee, you immediately jump into action. In order to soothe the hurt, you of course want to take steps to make things better and start the healing process. First, you assess the situation with loving attention. Then, you gently clean away any dirt or gravel. Next, you'll cover the wound, making a sheltered space for healing. Underneath the bandage, the body's genius goes to work immediately: fighting infection, growing new cells, reconnecting tissue. Kissing the bandage or brushing loving fingertips over the wound is the final step. We all know that love and connection increase the speed and depth of healing wounds, both big and small.

Of course, there are plenty of nonphysical wounds we all carry—persistent pain from long ago trauma, tender responses to present difficulties, or fear for an unknown future. In our modern world, these wounds take the form of pervasive anxiety, loneliness, stress, depression, and apathy.

What if we applied a creative process similar to the simple healing process above to address these psychic wounds? First, we might use awareness to see things as they really are, rather than as we think they should be. Then, we might cleanse away the dirt and gravel of social conditioning and self-judgment that muddy our healing. Next we can create a safe space, steeped in love and connection, so that natural mending can begin. Just as the body begins fighting infection, we can commit ourselves to rooting out negativity and criticism. Like the body grows new cells and reconnects tissue, so we might practice curiosity and bring our imagination into the process so that we can make new connections and open up new avenues for growth.

In short, creativity drives healing.

I know this because I've seen it happen again and again. For several years, in addition to my daily work as a writer and creative guide, I have taught an online class called Creative UnBootcamp. I envisioned this class as a place for people interested in writing to quickly tap into the creative process and shore up their writing skills.

Registering from all around the world, people showed up for the first session hungry to nourish a need much greater than learning how to write. This confused me at first. I was ready to teach the mechanics of putting words on the page, but the learners were bringing a whole lot more to the table: unexpressed emotions and desires, unresolved pain and yearning. *What did they want from this class? How could I be of service?*

The answer came almost by accident. Because the class was private, members could share their experiences with each other in a safe space in online chats. We were gathered in this intimate space even though we were spread out geographically. We had a place to explore and connect that was separate from our daily lives, families, jobs, and communities. On the surface, our task was to learn writing as a tool of self-expression, and stories came flooding out from the group immediately. In the privacy of our circle, members shared their traumas, their hidden longings, and their hopes and dreams. They revealed things they'd never told anyone before or had long since forgotten themselves. We laughed and cried together, writing long, ragged posts filled with profanity. The depth of honesty and trust they offered each other and me was humbling.

While this hadn't been my initial goal for the class, it was obvious that we had touched a nerve—a big one. The group was filling a need much greater than helping people gain a few writing skills.

Over the next few years of offering this course, my understanding evolved. I watched people gain confidence with new writing skills while at the same time opening up their creative self-expression. This resulted in an ever-expanding cycle, wherein self-discovery fueled creativity, and creativity in turn expanded new pathways of self-discovery. I further watched as this growth process blossomed into profound transformations in people's lives. This went beyond writing. It improved people's relationships at home and at work and enhanced their overall health, well-being, mood, and resilience.

Again and again, as I worked with hundreds of people in group settings and in one-on-one sessions, I saw a direct connection between consciously expressing our creativity and healing our lives.

That discovery has become the basis for this book.

Yet creativity can feel elusive and unattainable. Throughout my own life, I've often struggled to think of myself as creative and failed to nurture my own creativity. Why do we do this? Most simply, because we have been told (and have learned to tell ourselves) that we are "not creative," that creativity is a commodity or quality to be acquired, and that it's a scarce resource only a few special people we call artists can possess.

That story about creativity just isn't true.

So what is the truth?

Creativity is the process by which imagination becomes reality. It exists in bountiful supply within everyone and calls on our innate gifts of curiosity, attention, and loving connection so that we can live fuller and more meaningful lives.

When we uncover this truth about creativity and build a practice to discover and express our inner creative self, what follows is nothing short of total personal transformation.

Besides being fun, creativity offers a path out of stagnation, unhappiness, self-judgment, and the kind of robotic living that leaves so many of us feeling unfulfilled. Creativity is a forgotten cure for these life-depleting ailments and a spiritual practice for returning to your truest self and living a life you love.

My Story

Why do I feel that creativity can change your life? Because it saved mine.

By the time I was thirty-four, I had created a frightening mess of a life. On the outside, I was the successful CEO of a mortgage company, cofounder of two other ventures, and had just moved into a large, beautiful home with my then wife and our three young children. Meanwhile, I'd gained seventy pounds, slept only a handful of hours a night, and was buckling under the strain of keeping up a false persona that even my close friends believed was true. I was clinging to the role of "ambitious young entrepreneur living the dream," which I was never meant to play.

Having attained so much of what I had convinced myself I wanted, I could not begin to reconcile the hollowness, dread, and confusion I felt every moment of every day. The idea of confiding in someone else felt impossible, weak, and ridiculous.

During this time, I agreed to attend a meditation retreat focused on personal transformation. I didn't want to go, but looking back now, I think a deeply hidden voice, one I wasn't conscious of at the time, said yes to that invitation.

In one particular exercise, the leader of the retreat asked us to travel back to a time in our life when we felt free and to imagine an encounter with our younger self, face-to-face. Looking into the eyes of the child I had once been, I saw he was observing me with curiosity and sadness. He couldn't understand where my joy and passion for life had gone. It was as if he wanted to ask me, *Why did you do all of this? I never wanted a life of constant stress and anxiety—not for any reason, least of all money.* I started weeping, embarrassed that I could not control the flood of my emotions.

I returned to my life on Monday, but as a dear friend of mine says, once you know something, you can't unknow it. I now knew that I had created a life based on acquisition of stuff that was fueled by an inner fear of rejection, all in a futile attempt to live up to society's definition of success. I also knew it was quite literally killing me and that I couldn't do it much longer. Yet I was stuck, afraid to destroy what I had built. How could I walk away from my house, job, wife, or kids? I felt I would rather die.

That's when life stepped in to help.

Shortly after the retreat, the global financial crisis of 2008 unfolded, and in the process my business was washed away. I was *forced* to let go. I lost my house, retirement accounts, credit score, and pretty much everything that had become my identity. It was painful, humiliating, and terrifying.

It was also one of the best things that could have ever happened to me.

I had thought that losing everything was my biggest fear. As it turns out, I had a bigger fear, one that had driven my choices for a long while: a fear of just being me, of being *enough*, without stuff or accomplishments. Here I was, back to square one. And it was a relief.

This "disaster" gave me the chance to return to curiosity and innocence. I started asking real questions about life, my place in it, and what I might want from whatever time I had left on earth. I gazed back into the eyes of the passionate, spirited child I had been and decided I would follow his lead. I promised him

I would stop denying and repressing myself in order to get ahead. I didn't know it then, but this began the process of bringing my life back into alignment with who I really am.

After this outer collapse, I began an inner process of self-discovery, self-acceptance, and creative expression that has changed everything. Returning to my creative nature was the master key to this transformation. Healing my connection to this part of myself served as a model for healing the rest of my life—bringing me back from the verge of self-destruction and giving me a way to thrive, to enjoy and be inspired by life again.

What to Expect from This Book

This book will offer you a path back home to what I call your *inner creative self* and help you more fully express this in your life.

What do I mean by this phrase? Well, since creativity is the process by which imagination becomes reality, we can think of the inner creative self as the source of imagination. Creativity is the *action* that springs from this special place inside us.

Your inner creative self is like a part of your soul, and it has been with you from the beginning of your life. It's curious, open, and playful, delighting in new ideas, the joy of discovery, and the endless diversity of human expression. You may have forgotten about this part of you or learned to ignore it, but it can never die. Much like the concepts of the soul or the mind, it's hard to describe the inner creative self in words, even though it is an undeniable, essential part of each of us. It can be easier to experience it viscerally . . .

Think of a time you did something that engaged you so completely that you lost your sense of time or even of your own physical presence. It could be anything—chopping a pile of wood, building a delicate house of cards, or playing make-believe in the yard as a child. This is the feeling of being absorbed in a task, responsive, open, and integrated in mind, body, and heart.

In my experience, we can feel our inner creative self when we are fully engaged in this way in the present moment and expressing our creativity consciously. This state can certainly be achieved through traditional creative arts such as writing, painting, dancing, sculpting, singing, etc., but it's not limited to those pursuits. When it comes to creative expression, the possibilities are endless.

The trick is that we can't "think" our way into the inner creative self. It's more like a muscle that we can develop through active practice. This practice is creativity itself, a combination of how we look at the world and the actions we take to bring imagination into reality. This book is brimming with fun and useful ways to build your practice of creativity.

Some of these practices will be familiar to those who run in creative circles already, while others are more often used in areas of personal development and might not fit into your existing idea of creativity. In every case, I have tested them on myself for years and teach them to clients and those who attend my courses. Through these exercises and experiments, I have watched new insights pop on like light bulbs, illuminating the path to a deeper connection to self and lifelong creative exploration.

Call to mind your favorite artist, musician, writer, or painter. Anyone you love for their art has committed to their own inner creative being. They have honored the truth of their deepest selves, bringing it into the world through their own imagination. These artists seem not to care what people think as they express themselves in larger-than-life ways. They revel in activities that would make most of us feel shy or ridiculous.

We grant these people special latitude, saying they inhabit a plane of existence high in the rarified air of "artistic success." We celebrate their spontaneity and eccentricity. We hope they'll show us even more of themselves, right out in the open. Yet most of us are terrified to offer ourselves this same kind of freedom. We're dazzled by the beauty of someone living out their innermost creative desires, and meanwhile we wait for permission to explore the truth of who we really are.

We can feel the same freedom as the artists we admire; we can grant ourselves the same permission to be weird, wild, and wonderful. How? The key is to practice. Think of a sport. No novice can walk out their door and ski jump off a mountain or flip through a gymnastics routine. No amount of believing you can do those things by itself will make it happen. But you can teach the body and mind to achieve astounding feats, step-by-step. This is the promise of practice.

You have the right (I might even say the responsibility) to restore your creative function and to reclaim the spirituality, healing, and joy that belong to you. Please stop waiting for an invitation to be yourself. Start right now, right here, by diving into creative action and establishing your regular creative practice. It's easier than you think and also a whole lot of fun.

Having a regular creative practice sends a powerful wake-up call to your inner creative self, which in turn begins to work its magic on every aspect of your life, imbuing everything from mundane tasks to your highest calling with curiosity and possibility. You reconnect to the love of experience and playfulness and find they are inexhaustible resources. You rediscover the joy of creating. You begin to fall in love with life again.

My hope for all of us is that we can approach life with the eyes and heart of an artist; with the courage to transform anything that is painful or not working through this practice of creative imagination. Remember that skinned knee? Assessing with clear eyes, making space for nurturing and growth, providing loving shelter: this is the healing that creativity can bring to your true self—the self you're learning to know, accept, and love.

Let's begin.

One

Your Creative Birthright

The artist is not a special kind of person;
rather each person is a special kind of artist.
—Ananda Coomaraswamy

When I tell people that I am a writer and creative guide, I tend to hear the response, "Oh, that sounds interesting," often followed by, "I'm just not that creative," or "I've never been a creative person." I often perceive a note of regret in these statements, even loneliness, as if these folks were missing out on a special club they don't deserve to join.

Nothing could be further from the truth—and yet this sentiment is widespread, which perplexes me. How could something as intrinsic as creativity be silenced by the unholy mantra of "I'm not creative"?

Perhaps you have thought or even spoken these words aloud.

It seems that most nonartists—that is, people who don't regularly paint, write, perform, or do other traditional arts—have this tape playing in their minds.

Even for those of us who have always known we are creative (in the traditional sense and beyond), if we look closely, we find a belief running in the background that says, "I'm not creative enough."

That's why I want to begin by reclaiming the word *creativity* and broaden our notion of who belongs in this club. Painters, writers, singers, actors, and the like are creative, of course, but I know this to be true at the core of my being: *every human being is creative.*

Look around the room you're in right now. Everything in it owes at least part of its existence to the creative process. From the books on the shelves, to the gentle curve of a vase, to the color painted on the walls—a human being used their imagination to shape reality. Expand your awareness further and think of skyscrapers, interconnected telecom systems, formal gardens, viral videos, or regional cuisines. The examples are endless; the world we occupy has been built by creative endeavors.

Creativity is your birthright. You were born possessing this quality. Even if you have lost or forgotten about certain aspects of your inner creative self, every breath and heartbeat can be a new opportunity to reclaim and develop this elemental part of you. In a deeper sense, I believe that each of us is meant to be an artist of life itself, shaping and creating every part of living into a work of art that reflects our true desires and whole selves.

This book is an invitation to come back home to yourself in two ways. First, by building a creative practice that revitalizes your creative birthright. And second, by teaching you to channel this creative power into other areas of your life, such as your job, your home, your relationships with others, and, most importantly, your relationship with yourself.

Even if you don't believe it yet, this point bears repeating: Every human is creative. There is no such thing as an uncreative human. My hope is that by the end of this book you will claim this truth for yourself and make it your new mantra:

I am creative. I am an artist. I am creating my life.

Not only are you fundamentally creative, but you can exercise the muscle of your inner creative self. Simply saying this mantra a few times a day is a good start. The power of a mantra is that it works on your subconscious, so that even if you don't fully believe what you are saying, you are practicing the belief until it becomes true for you.

It may not yet feel true. That's okay. If creativity is in fact built into our DNA, as I believe is the case, how can so many people think that they're not creative or not creative enough? Where did we go off track? As with any new understanding or shift in perspective, we'll need to start with awareness.

If you travel back far enough in the memories of your childhood, you will likely find a version of yourself that saw things in a creative way and naturally expressed the creative impulse without even thinking about it. Results from a creativity test built for NASA by Dr. George Land showed that five-year-olds earned the highest marks of any group, scoring 98 percent. That's because as children we drew, painted, made things, played make-believe, explored, experimented, and had a looser adherence to standard rules and systems. Kids can help us reactivate our own creativity. Have you ever played "the floor is lava"? The rules are simply those four words—pretend the floor is hot lava and you can't touch it. Everyone immediately suspends their disbelief, leaping from chair to couch, in a matter of moments upending every rule about how we "should" behave in our living rooms.

Somewhere along the way, we traded this immersive creativity for logic, predictability, correctness, and responsibility. Our educational system, built at the dawn of the industrial revolution and largely unchanged today, churns out workers fit for factories, stamping out creativity on purpose. Perhaps someone told you "you're not that creative" or "your art is no good," and you believed them. You may also have experienced something traumatic, which understandably shut down your creative self, as you had to prioritize survival over imagination.

The Enemies of Creativity

Part of reversing this process is to become aware of your own habits and blocks and learn how they got there. By bringing awareness to these enemies of creativity, you can overcome them and begin to build new habits and practices in their place. To that end, let's look at the three primary forces that come together to dampen our creative impulses and divorce us from our inner creative self:

- Socialization

- Traumatic experiences

- Rejection

I will cover these in greater depth later in the book, and we'll explore how to move beyond them, but here's a snapshot of what I mean in each instance.

Socialization

Socialization is the process by which we become functioning members of society. It's how we learn to communicate with each other, behave as part of a cohesive group, and navigate within the complex social worlds we inhabit. Like so many tools, socialization can be both a positive and negative force. By the time we reach adulthood, our beliefs, behaviors, tastes, and personal goals often align with socialized norms and no longer feel like extensions of our true creative selves. We may lose sight of where we end and society begins, creating a sense of alienation from ourselves. We may begin to believe that we are broken or "not enough." Trying to regain a sense of belonging, we go further into the cycle of trying to adhere to social structures, cutting us off from our innate creativity even more.

Traumatic Experiences

Trauma is a highly sensitive topic, especially for those who have experienced severe episodes. Even for those who haven't felt trauma at an extreme level, this enemy of creativity remains relevant, since everybody has lived through traumatic experiences of some kind, such as divorce, bullying, loss of a loved one, or illness. The nervous system reacts to trauma with a survival response, scaling back to the basic functions housed in the brain stem: fight, flight, or freeze. In order to be creative, we need to have the physical and psychological safety to use our whole brain and being freely, so trauma literally stifles creativity on a cellular level. If we experience trauma, especially in our formative years, it can lead to patterns of anxiety, destructive self-talk, inner criticism, procrastination, perfectionism, addictive behaviors, self-doubt, or feelings of being not valuable or lacking a purpose.

Rejection

Rejection sits at the intersection of socialization and trauma. Like it or not, violating the written or unwritten rules of our families, religion, or society at large can lead to rejection of all kinds, which is a traumatic experience in its own right. Sociologists tell us that the fear of being rejected can be nearly as strong as the fear of death. After all, for most of human history, being banished from one's group meant facing the terrors of nature alone, which was tantamount to death. Some of us grew up in punitive environments where we were told "you can't do it" or "you're not enough," further squelching natural curiosity and the ability to take creative risks. We learned from many well-meaning caregivers to doubt who we are and what we are capable of.

The biggest threat that rejection poses to our creativity is a learned resistance to making mistakes and failing. Failure is an essential element of experimentation, growth, and creative expression. We have to be able to try new things. Rejection tells us that there is a "right" way, and that your value is tied to your ability to get it right. Yet if you study the history of any individual who achieved something we value today, they walked a tough road of rejections and setbacks. We only accept and cheer their individuality after the fact. For many of us, this fear of rejection is so palpable that it stymies our creative thinking and expression by whispering in quiet voices, *Don't be different. Don't try something new. Don't get it wrong.*

Together, socialization, traumatic experiences, and rejection work to shut down our inner creative self over the course of our lives. Over time, the individuality and wholeness we enjoy thanks to our creative nature are replaced with its opposite: *conformity*.

While these three enemies of creativity join forces and appear to be a formidable wall of opposition, the good news is that your creative nature remains intact beneath any layers of socialization, rejection, and trauma you may have experienced. There are many ways to move through and beyond these obstacles, and we will explore them in depth in these pages. This doesn't have to be a long, arduous process, either. One of the most exciting things about creativity, to me, is its special power to turn a whole system or way of thinking on its head in a single moment of delight, awe, or surprise.

What if a practice existed you could do every day that gave you more energy, made daily life more fun and interesting, helped others, revealed new approaches to old problems, and connected you more deeply to your innermost hopes and dreams? Of course you'll know by now that I'm talking about creativity. As important as food, water, and shelter, creativity sustains and gives us life.

This book doesn't stop at giving you some ideas to be more creative. Rather, it seeks to energize your connection to the natural creative impulse that exists in all of life. After all, you yourself are the greatest creative product you can offer the world. Anything you bring forward into the world from your inner creative self will be rare, valuable, and original.

My hope is that by the time you finish reading this book, you will have established a personal creative practice that can last the rest of your life. This practice will build your creative capacity, transform your core beliefs about yourself, and heal your connection to your inner artist.

You don't need to add anything to your life or fix anything about yourself. Creativity is your birthright, and this book is designed to help you remember that. We are not healing the creative nature. It is already whole and healthy, hidden or buried though it may be. We are simply healing our *connection* to this critical part of our being—our ability to live more deeply in it and to express it in every area of our lives. Once the connection is healed, you can take this artfulness and spirit of creativity back to your work, your home, your social circles, and everywhere else you go.

Even if you don't yet believe it yourself, I know this is true in the marrow of my bones: you are an artist, and your life is your unfolding, ever-changing masterpiece.

Key Tools for Developing a Creative Connection

In my personal experience and in working with others, I have found that our inner creative self holds the key to literally everything our heart desires. However, since so many of us were forced to abandon ourselves in some capacity early on, our connection to this inner self has grown weak and full of static. Two key tools will help us throughout this process of finding and developing this weakened connection to our inner creative self: meditation and journaling.

Meditation builds the awareness and self-acceptance we need to clear the signal, and journaling boosts the power and turns up the volume, so that creativity can flow out of us without judgment. Of course, there are other concrete benefits to these practices you may have heard about, including greater peace of mind, mental clarity, reduced anxiety, and even health benefits like lowered blood pressure.

I know that despite these benefits, some of you reading this have tried to do one or both of these before and didn't stick with it. Others might feel angst at the mere suggestion of trying either one. If this describes you, I can relate. I once felt itchy even thinking about sitting in silence or writing about my feelings.

If this sounds like you, I would simply ask that you keep an open mind to both at this point. The kind of journaling and meditation I will suggest might be easier and more enjoyable than you think.

Let's look at each of these practices individually.

Journaling

In this book I'm going to invite you to try a new approach to journaling, one I call the "Creative Self journal." This type of journaling is designed to foster a rich conversation with yourself—and can provide you with a wealth of surprising benefits:

- Get reacquainted with your inner creative self.

- Process questions, anxieties, and issues in your life in a safe, private place without judgment or competition.

- Acknowledge and articulate your wants and needs, and nurture the dreams and hopes that fuel them.

My life has grown steadily better as I have established and maintained this journaling practice over the years. I've noticed myself get clearer, stronger, less anxious, more open to new ideas and perspectives, and more able to state my needs and move in the direction of my dreams. In short, I feel more connected to the voice of my inner creative self and more empowered to follow where it leads.

I've watched this happen time and time again to those I work with as a guide. Using this practice regularly leads to surprising clarity and improvement, often in areas that have been seriously tangled or painful for a long time.

With such clear benefits, why can it be so difficult to take up this practice? When I bring up the topic of journaling, here are some of the biggest objections I hear:

1. "I'm not a writer." / "I don't like to write."

2. "I don't have time to write."

3. "When I try to journal, the only thing that comes out is boring, whiny, barfy drivel."

Here are my responses: You don't have to like writing in order to benefit from journaling. No one is going to read anything you don't want to share. You don't have to compose monumental epics here. This is just jotting down your thoughts, that's all, and I will be giving you simple prompts so you'll never have to think of what to write.

Plus, we're all writers. One way or another, I bet you write something every day: emails, text messages, reports, posts on social media, lists, and more. Remember, we're reclaiming the titles of creativity for everyone. We're all artists.

Additionally, when it comes to finding the time to write, please know that you can journal for any length of time and see results, even just a few minutes a day. Journaling can be done while you have your morning cup of coffee. It can be done in the few minutes between brushing your teeth and turning out the light to go to bed at night. It can be done on a ten-minute break at work. Getting ready to watch a five-minute YouTube video of champion ballroom dancing? Journal instead (and then go ahead and watch the video—professional ballroom dancing is awesome).

And finally, while I doubt what you write comes out as boring, whiny, barfy drivel, your journal is the exact right place for the kind of cathartic brain dumping that can clear the way for fresh and exciting creative expression. Many people I know who practice creativity every day have piles of material they consider to be drivel (whether anyone would agree with them or not); it's a natural, organic, positive part of the creative process. The barfier, the better.

I'll be offering small prompts for you to answer throughout this book. These are designed to pique your curious nature and stimulate your creativity. Many of my students surprise themselves with what comes out in response to these prompts and marvel at their own ability to write and express their thoughts and feelings.

At the end of this chapter, we will take the first steps to start our creative self journaling practice.

Meditation

Just as creativity may seem to be reserved for traditional artists, many of us see meditation as something meant for spiritual gurus or Buddhist monks. I know that I did for many years, and this belief—along with my perfectionistic hang-ups—made it difficult to start practicing what has become a vital connection to my life, and life itself. If you think about it, believing that only spiritual adepts can enjoy the benefits of meditation would be like saying that exercise should be reserved for elite Olympic athletes.

Just like exercise, meditation can take any number of forms. It's not just about sitting silently in a room. You can practice active meditation by walking in the wilderness or at the park, listening to your favorite music, or doing any other activity that brings you into quiet awareness and introspection. Even exercise itself can be a form of meditation—hiking, jogging, yoga, and tai chi are good examples.

The difference between doing any of these activities on their own and doing them as a meditative practice centers on what's going on inside you. The intent here is to build awareness of things as they are—not as you think they should be or remember they used to be. Accepting things as they are becomes a powerful antidote to self-criticism, judgment, and competition. Awareness brings you out of the anxious state that creates inner static and doesn't allow you to feel safe and receive.

Want to know who meditates regularly? Some of the most influential, creative people on the planet—Sir Paul McCartney, Oprah Winfrey, and Tom Hanks, to name just a few. Jerry Seinfeld meditates twice daily and credits his practice of over forty years with helping him maintain the endless energy and original ideas he needed while creating *Seinfeld* and his youthfulness since then, explaining that "meditation is like a phone charger for your body and mind."

Both of these practices—journaling and meditation—will be key as you do the work of unraveling socialization, rejection, and trauma. They put you back in touch with your creative nature, quiet your inner critic, and rekindle joy in your life.

To help inspire you to begin these two key practices, here are some exercises that can get you started.

Exercise: Acquiring Your Journal

The first step to writing in a journal is to choose or make one just for this purpose.

There are countless options out there for purchasing a new blank journal to write in, but take a few moments before you begin looking to consider what would work best for you here. If you like to doodle or draw and you know your journal will contain a lot of this, why not consider a blank sketchbook instead of a lined journal? Do you like the feel of small, compact books that you can stash in your bag and take with you on the road? Or do you prefer the peaceful practice of sitting down to a special desk and opening up a substantial book with wide, empty pages? Or maybe you'd like both: a small notepad for thoughts and dreams dashed out on the fly and a bigger book to elaborate on those notes later when you have the time.

Consider also that you could make your own book (there are a number of tutorials online for creating your own handmade journals) or perhaps just embellish and decorate the cover of a purchased book with doodles, drawings, and collage. This is your book, and it can be as simple or as elaborate as you wish. The important thing here is that your journal should attract you . . . make you want to pick it up and get scribbling! That will mean something different for everyone. For me, it means I need something simple and cheap. I want it to feel temporary so that I don't ever worry about messing it up or making it presentable for someone else. That keeps me from getting too precious. For other friends and students, a more decorative approach feels more attractive. They want to spend time with something beautiful that incorporates their favorite colors and textures.

Whatever you choose, your journal is and will continue to be an amazing conduit for your inner creative self. Over time, you may choose to keep photographs, drawings, and other memorabilia in your journal, and it will grow and evolve and change with you on your journey.

I journal in a physical book and write by hand with a pen or pencil rather than typing on a computer or phone. Writing by hand isn't essential, but it does allow your brain to slow down. By doing something that feels unfamiliar or even awkward, you are breaking out of your accustomed mental patterns, which allows for new insights and creative ideas to show up. Additionally, you access different parts of your brain and experience more of the sensory spectrum when writing by hand—the sound of the pen scratching on paper, the weight of the journal in your hand, etc.

However, if you have physical pain or limitations that make writing by hand impossible, definitely find the best journaling method for you. I have a friend, for example, who has both a physical and an electronic journal, as she feels that the speed of typing allows her to access a sense of creative movement and flow that is different from handwriting. Some of my clients use voice journals or recording apps on their phones and find that this helps them.

I don't believe in a specific dogma about how journaling must be done. The point of this experience is to allow space and time to heal the connection to your inner creative self!

Exercise: Practicing a Simple Meditation

Meditation doesn't have to include special postures, cushions, bells, singing bowls, or a committed meditation room or space. You can meditate right now where you are for just a few minutes. Every moment you spend focused on the present, on your breath, on stillness and peace, will calm and center you and open your whole being to its creative potential.

Here's just one example of a simple, short exercise you can do right now to get a taste of how meditation can improve your mental well-being.

Begin by connecting with your body and surroundings. Find a quiet place where you can be sure to be undisturbed for at least a few minutes. You can sit on the floor or in a chair with your feet on the floor.

Place your hands on your knees, then take three slow, deep breaths in and out. Now slowly raise and lower each finger, one at a time, starting with your left pinkie and moving across to the fingers of your right hand in sequence. Focus your attention on each finger as you raise and lower it.

Now lift the toes of your right foot and stretch them as far as they can go while counting to five. Do the same with your left toes. Breathe gently with each movement—in and out. This whole exercise should take two to three minutes. You can do this at your desk, in your car while you're waiting for traffic to move, or even during a meeting. Taking the time to breathe, focus, and count slows your mind, brings your attention back into your body, and calms anxiety.

Once you've done the exercise at least once, check in with yourself. Do you feel more connected to the moment than you did before? More calm? Relaxed? If the answer is no, repeat the exercise if you have time. Meditation and mindfulness become even more relaxing and powerful with regular practice.

Two

Joy and the Art of Self-Discovery

Joy is but the sign that creative emotion is fulfilling its purpose.
—Charles Du Bos

It is said that when Zeus wanted to locate the center of Grandmother Earth, or Gaia, he sent two eagles flying from the farthest points east and west, and at the point the eagles crossed each other, he established Delphi, placing an egg-shaped stone there to symbolize the navel of the world. The builders of the ancient Temple of Apollo at Delphi inscribed this maxim into the stone at its entrance: "Know thyself."

For eons, self-knowledge has provided the foundation for the work of thinkers, philosophers, and spiritual teachers around the world. Lao Tzu, the great teacher of Taoist principles, said this: "Knowing others is intelligence; knowing yourself is true wisdom." Self-knowledge might seem tricky to access and hold on to, but the rewards of doing this deep work are many. Finding out who you really are and what you really want is the most fulfilling thing you can ever do.

How can we find out who we really are? We can start by cutting out what doesn't matter, what isn't true for us, and then begin to bring coherence to our inner and outer worlds. Being out of alignment causes suffering, consumes our energy, and degrades our health. As you discover yourself and align your life so that it becomes an expression of who you really are, you find that creativity and vitality well up like a mountain spring from this center place.

When you embark on the lifelong journey of knowing yourself, your whole life can become a work of art. If it's difficult to connect with such an ideal state, I suggest what has helped me: begin to practice artfulness in small moments. Our inner creative selves seek expression in all of life, not just in the grand gestures. As you experience the tiny spark that accompanies any brush with your creative nature, you will find yourself inspired to do more of that.

It might feel difficult to begin this journey of creative self-discovery, burdened as we are with past traumatic experiences and layers of societal expectations. So I'd like to offer a guiding light, a north star that never fails to draw me onward, reorient my progress, and brighten my path.

This is a principle, an image to keep in mind, a feeling, a friend and teacher. What is the name of this mentor-muse?

Joy. Her name is Joy.

We know her already, for we met her in our first moments on earth. We relished her presence as children, before we knew what to call her, before we had any words at all. Joy is the essence, the fuel, and the energy of the creative life.

So many of us have lost track of joy, seeking instead the acceptance of others. Afraid of failure and rejection, we try to live the life others want us to live or become who others told us to be and acquire what others told us we should want. Even in these pursuits, if we look back, we can see that we started them innocently, because we thought they would bring us joy.

Of course, joy doesn't depend on piles of wealth or the acceptance of our peers or parents. Anyone watching kids play can see that. Joy can be embraced even in the midst of pain and adversity. Meanwhile, its opposite, despair, consumes the lives and hearts of countless "successful" people.

When we understand that joy will guide us to everything we truly want in life, it can become the muse that moves us along in the direction of our dreams and desires. Joy becomes a wise mentor, guiding us through perils and hardships, helping us make the hard choices that are sometimes necessary to stay on the path.

Here's the thing: joy and creativity go together. One way to look at it is like this: Joy is your guide, and creativity is the method by which you travel.

How does this work? One way to think of it is that joy and creativity will show you the simplest path toward your heart's deepest desires. You can learn the habit of asking yourself what will bring you joy and then pursuing that thing. Whether it's the simple delight of a morning coffee outside or the profound wonder of exploring a part of the world that's new to you, pursuing joy will help you decide what's important for you and what doesn't matter at all. In this way, joy can show you the shortest distance between two points: where you are and where you want to go. Being creative, or turning your life into a work of art, is the means to get there.

I love the French phrase *joie de vivre*, "the joy of living." I experience this feeling when I am being creative, sensing the energy of life, love, and connection with my deepest self—even for a few seconds at a time. When you are completely engrossed in creating something, whether it's a soup for the evening meal or putting paint on a canvas, you have found a moment of joy.

Feelings Are Powerful

Our educational system teaches us to value logic over emotions. While this will help us in some situations, an overemphasis on logic can lead us to distrust our feelings and to discount the decision-making acumen of our emotions.

I want to introduce the idea that feelings are powerful, an essential fact that we will revisit later in this book. For now, take a moment to honor the power of feelings. Anger can reveal your passion and protective instincts. Fear can warn you of danger, but also point you toward areas of potential growth. Joy can lead you back to your creative self. So many of us were raised to accept a widespread cultural suspicion and disregard for feelings, so we never learned to follow their nuanced guidance. In my experience, emotions can be the colorful, sensual, insightful messages sent out from our true self. We can learn to tune in to them and consciously harness them as creative fuel in every area of life.

In my own case, as a young child I was bursting with energy and excitement. I would wake up so full of life that I couldn't wait to run outside and climb the apricot tree or plan the launch of a new night crawler bait stand with my brother. I remember one day, when I was ten years old, I walked into the living room one evening after reading my favorite book for the two hundredth time and declared to my parents,

"I'm going to be a writer." They both smiled warmly and said, "That's wonderful!" I glowed. I knew for sure what I wanted to become, and it would be a vocation born of pure joy.

And then I forgot. I grew up, and life brought the responsibilities of bills to pay and children to feed. Somewhere along the line I heard that all writers starve unless they are very lucky. I began to believe it, and I found evidence for this "fact" everywhere I looked. Having grown up in poverty, I knew I would never willingly choose that struggle for myself or my children.

It's not entirely true to say that I forgot my dream of being a writer, but it sank into the background. Every once in a while I would write something, give it to someone to read, and they would say, "That touched me. You have a gift." The feeling I had as a kid would return—the joy, the glow. Then I would remind myself that I needed to earn $10 million so that I could buy my freedom to write. I felt I needed to be successful before I could follow my dream, but I had no idea what that word *success* really meant to me. I knew what it meant to others, though, and to society at large, so I adopted other people's goals and ideals, never imagining that my own dream could lead me to real success.

Two and a half decades later, I found myself wrung dry of joy. I had lost the feeling of love and elation in my own life, and I didn't know how to find my way back. By believing a false narrative about success, I totally missed the opportunity to harness the power of joy to create the life I longed for as an adult.

Joy and Vulnerability

In order to experience joy, you must be willing and able to feel deeply. Perhaps you've recognized this feeling in the tender, naked glow right after you're done making love. In those moments of emotional and physical nakedness with another, we are open to the slightest breeze or twitch of feeling. Our psychological nerve endings are exposed and we are porous—able to receive nourishment at a deep level. We are also open to hurt and misunderstanding. Nothing is hidden, and we don't have the usual control of our shields, defenses, and faculties. That's why feeling joy can also make you so vulnerable—you're using the same emotional muscle that feels difficult emotions.

The state of joy is our most creative zone; it is also our least guarded. This is why past rejection and traumatic experiences can lead us to close ourselves off, to shut down our vulnerability. The problem is that when we do this, we also close ourselves off to joy. Once we have sustained traumatic injury to our trusting nature, opening back into this original state of joy can prove difficult.

I traded my pursuit of joy for what I thought was success. Sadly, many people who have achieved high levels of outward success have done the same. If this describes you, then I invite you to change your definition of success, to something more like this:

Success is the ability to cultivate and experience joy in all aspects of your life.

On the surface, this seems to diverge drastically from most popular beliefs about success and happiness. Would this definition of success be possible for you? Would it be worth working toward with the same drive and focus with which you build a career or a financial portfolio? Could it make you happier, healthier, more creative, and more connected to the people and things you love than you are today?

That's exactly what this definition does for me.

Following my joy has led me back to life one step at a time. From the smallest preference (what would I enjoy for lunch?) to the most life-changing concern (what legacy will I leave when I'm gone?), I had a new question to orient me: "Where's my joy?" This question helped me through years of healing and recovery. It was the guide that assisted in the often-difficult process of deciding what could stay and what must be cleared from my life.

The idea of joy as a compass pointing the way to real success is so foreign to most people that when I bring it up in my work as a creative guide, I hear all sorts of reactions. Most people believe that choosing joy would make them fall into personal ruin or would make them silly or irresponsible. Nothing could be further from the truth. Pursuing joy doesn't make you naive, a sucker, or a freeloader. In fact, I would argue that fear makes you far more likely to become these things. I offer my clients the question of joy to use as a guiding principle because I believe that their own joy is sane and wise.

In my view, each of us holds our own unique answers inside us to the great questions of life, and the job of any guide, myself included, is to help you remember what you already know. If I could wave a wand over your head and restore you to the ultimate state of creativity, I would simply say the magic words, "Remember joy."

Remembering joy—how it feels and how to express it—is the shortest distance between where you are now and where you want to go.

Be prepared, however, that reclaiming joy isn't always easy. Many people have shut down joy so long ago that they struggle to remember how it felt, and new joy feels squarely outside their comfort zone. Finding or remembering what brings them joy can feel impossible. If you feel lost when it comes to joy, please allow yourself to trust that you *can* heal your capacity for joy. It may take some time, but you really can. I'm living proof.

This book includes a wide range of simple practices designed to get you back in touch with your inner joy—and fostering creativity is a key source of joy.

Exercise: Three Questions

The following three questions are a simple and gentle way for you to hear the voice of your inner creative self again and help you reconnect to your joy. These are simple on purpose, and if you have a tendency to overthink things (as I do), I'd say go ahead and just try this with an open mind for now.

By now you have acquired or made your first creative self journal, so grab it and a pen, plus a cup of tea or coffee, and put on some great music. If you feel stuck or worried about starting to write, I encourage you to remind yourself of the things we discussed about writing in the last chapter. You may find it helpful to say these out loud as you sit down to write:

- *I am a writer*. I can write to myself and express my feelings, needs, desires, and ideas clearly.

- *I'm writing this only for myself and to myself.*
  It's not for anyone else to see, approve of, or
  criticize.

- *I don't need any validation from others in this
  space.* I am learning to be my own best friend
  and ally.

Question One: What am I feeling right now?

Begin by describing any feelings you have at this
moment, perhaps including frustration with the process of writing these things down. You get to be ter-
ribly honest here; no need to be lofty, profound, wise,
or kind. Let anything come out that wants to come
out. If you feel bored, anxious, tired, afraid, curious,
happy, sad . . . say so. Let it all pour out on the page.

You might feel moved to include physical sensations you're having—describe any discomforts or pain,
or talk about the small things in your immediate environment that feel good. For example, "I feel my butt
nestled solidly in the chair here at Neckar Coffee Shop.
My head aches a little because I stayed up too late last
night, but the steam from my coffee is a promise that
something hot and good will help . . ."

Many of us are so disconnected from our physical selves that beginning with a few lines about what's
going on around us can help us feel more grounded as

we go further into the practice. Try running through a checklist of your senses: what do you see, smell, feel, taste, and hear? Remember, *nothing is too small or too silly to write about*. Just be honest with yourself.

Now answer the question as it relates to your inner world. Maybe you're wrestling with a tough relationship issue—a hurting friendship or romantic partnership, something with a parent or sibling, a worry about one of your children, or something interpersonal at work. Talk about it. Describe what you're feeling right now, and let go of any impulse to edit or "make sense" of what you're feeling.

Question Two: What do I need right now?

Just as in the first question, it's most important to tell the truth. Many of us are not in the habit of saying—or even knowing—our needs. This often started in early childhood, when a parent or caregiver (probably unintentionally) communicated to our young psyches that our needs were unimportant, or even wrong. As a result, many of us feel that having needs isn't safe, and it can take some time and dedicated effort to dismantle this belief.

Begin to answer the question, "What do I need right now?" Start small and be honest. It might be something as simple as, "I need to pee." I suggest that you jump up and do that first, before anything else happens. The practice of paying attention to your needs, acknowledging them, and meeting them as quickly as possible is surprisingly therapeutic. Strange as it may seem, listening and responding to needs of any kind reinforce the process of healing your connection to your inner creative self.

Please be honest about your larger needs, too. For example, "I need money right now" or "I need a new car" or "I need a friend—someone I can trust. Someone with whom I feel safe, seen, and heard."

Again, don't worry if these two questions or your answers to them feel trivial. They are meant to get you started, and it doesn't matter where you start because all roads can lead you home to your inner creative self. Expressing the smallest, most shallow seeming anxiety or desire can be a thread that unravels a larger, knottier issue in your life.

Question Three: What would I love?

This is a magical question. It builds on the awareness of the first question and the reciprocity of the second question. This one has the power to shift you into a state of creative possibility and imagination. I use it often in my personal practice, and I take some time with all of my clients to explore this question at some point in their journey.

Here's how it works. Look back at what you've written so far, and pick one of the items that presented a challenge from questions 1 and 2. Then ask yourself, "What would I love?" Write down your answers without judgment or skepticism, no matter how unlikely or outlandish they might seem. Whether you would love another cup of coffee or would love to fly away into the sky, the point of this question is to simply allow yourself to state what you would love in any given situation. Please don't self-edit!

Writing the words "I would love . . ." along with an outcome or feeling you desire activates your imagination in a positive way.

Some people believe that we become less imaginative as we get older, but I know for sure that we don't lose it—rather, we are trained to stop imagining. From a young age, many of us are told to "grow up," or to "stop daydreaming," and are taught to be realistic and watch out for risks.

We can't lose our imagination entirely, so we train it to paint fearful scenes of what we *don't* want—the downside, the failure, the missed opportunity, the pain of disappointed dreams.

This third question invites you to let yourself imagine from a perspective of love and joy, opening up the power of your subconscious mind to turn your choices, behavior, and focus toward what you want to have happen rather than what you fear.

If you're having trouble with this prompt, try asking this question a different way: "How would I love to feel?" Especially if you're in a whirlwind of confusion, anxiety, or insecurity, asking how you'd love to feel can offer a new pathway. Maybe the answer is, "I would love to feel calm and centered right now. I would just love to feel safe." You can follow up with, "How would that feel in my body?" You might imagine feeling your shoulders drop, deep breaths coming in and out easily, and you'll naturally start taking small actions such as stretching, opening your lungs, and relaxing your muscles. You can build on these actions with a simple mantra such as, "I am safe. I am lovable. I am resourceful." Investigating how I would love to feel often leads me in the direction of feeling that way—that's the power of the creative imagination.

As you tune in to yourself in this way, you honor the anxiety, depression, anger, pain, or whatever else you're feeling and clarify for yourself what you need right now. This third question transforms these difficult feelings by opening up to what you most desire. With a little consistency, this practice accrues over time. If you are willing to be patient and gentle with yourself for ten minutes per day over the course of a few weeks and then months, your life will change.

Using this simple pattern of questions, you can't help but heal and strengthen your relationship with your inner creative self. As this happens, you may notice that your daily sessions become more and more enjoyable, like a conversation with a best friend who never gets tired of listening to you, no matter how often you repeat the same things, day after day. This friend is wise and kind. This friend is *you*. Your inner creative self longs to become your ally in generating a life that you love.

———

Once you've taken time to do this first journaling exercise, we will continue our exploration with a closer look at the enemies of creativity we talked about in the introduction and dive deeper into how they conspire to block us from our inner creative self. By understanding how these forces work, we can learn to break them down and move beyond them with confidence and purpose.

Three

Restoring Imagination

You can't depend on your eyes when
your imagination is out of focus.
—Mark Twain

I love the story of a high school teacher who drew a dot on the chalkboard and asked her students to identify it. They responded with the obvious: "It's a chalk dot."

The next day, the teacher asked a colleague to repeat the experiment, only this time in a classroom full of kindergarteners. They shouted out nonstop examples of what the dot might be: the top of a telephone pole, a squashed bug, an owl's eye, a black hole, a rotten egg, a seed, a baby dinosaur, and on and on.

Of course, no one could fault the "right answer" given by the high schoolers. Yet the responses of the five-year-olds were far more imaginative, not to mention entertaining. Our education system teaches us to see things in a fixed way, to look for the right answer and be ready to regurgitate it at the proper moment. There's a time and a place for this in life and work, of course. I want to get my exact change at the grocery store, and I want the technician processing my blood work to know just what they're looking at. But what a profound loss if that same clerk and lab worker can't access the infinite possibilities of a chalk dot in other areas of their lives.

This is partly how our connection to our inner creative self frays over time. As we grow older, we tend to trade imagination for logic, and like any other skill we don't use, we get out of practice using our imagination. Before long, we're looking at every situation and circumstance in our life from a single possibility rather than many. When we come to a difficult question or complex situation, we often double down on "being right," abandoning the gifts of curiosity, playfulness, and creativity that might lead to innovative solutions. In my experience we function best and get the most satisfaction out of life when we employ a healthy balance of logic and imagination.

Every human creation on earth began in someone's imagination. Whether it's the car you drive, the clothing you wear, the book or device you are using to read these words, or the city you live in or near—all of it started with a seed of imagination watered by the creative process.

What is this creative conception we call imagination? The word itself comes from the Latin root *imaginari*, which means "to picture oneself." Imagination is a kind of *seeing*, the ability to envision something that is not physically present for the eyes to see, or to put yourself in a different place than you are, using your senses in a hypothetical way.

Imagination is *personal*—each of us does it differently (though it can be done in groups with exciting results). It is *internal*—we don't need any outside tools or help to do it. And it's *intentional*—we do it on purpose. That is, imagining doesn't just happen to us, though we can be taught to do it unconsciously.

In the creative process, feelings and desires are the fuel, and imagination provides the muscle—the machinery of new ideas and resources. Imagination really is a muscle we can strengthen at any time in our lives, as we practice the habit of seeing in new ways.

When I tell people that creativity requires imagination, they nod their heads as if to say, "Okay, that's obvious . . ." Yet I'm always surprised by how many adults don't use their imagination much at all, let alone apply it in ways that could explode their capacity for joy and well-being.

That's not surprising when you consider how many of us, either in our formative years or as young adults, heard things like, "stop daydreaming," "it's time to grow up," or "be realistic." Or how about this one: "That's just your imagination." This last one has the double effect of discounting a gut feeling you may be having *and* devaluing the potential power of your imagination!

There's a way to be both grounded and wildly imaginative, to be creative and responsible, to day-dream and reach your goals. Unfortunately, this isn't the norm for most people. Nearly all of us get herded into adulthood by parents, teachers, and other well-meaning adults who try to teach us the discipline and skills they think we need to survive in the world. This happens through the process of socialization, and many of us have set aside the productive use of our imagination to appease its demands. Worse than that, socialization has a specialized tool that shuts down imagination every time: in order to enforce the power of social norms that don't feel right for us, we have to believe that we are not good enough just as we are.

Socialization: The Enemy of Imagination

Socialization is the process of acquiring social skills and learning cultural norms and customs so that we can become functioning members of society. Learning to speak, read, and use the toilet are all basic examples of skills learned through socialization.

The feeling of belonging and being a part of a group is essential to our mental and physical health, as well as to our development as a species. But here's the trouble: socialization doesn't stop with the basics. We form various tribes throughout life whose rules dictate everything we do, say, and prefer, from clothing and hairstyles to speech, recreational preferences, and career options. S. E. Hinton's novel *The Outsiders* illustrates life-and-death battles between the working-class Greasers and the upper-class Socials. If you were born to blue-collar parents, you didn't get to kiss a girl from the other side of the tracks. It might get you killed.

In my view, one of the most destructive ideas planted in humans through socialization is the notion that we are somehow broken or "not enough." In fact, this belief forms the foundation for the glass prison of socialization.

Consider the core message behind all the advertising and marketing that hits our eyes and ears on a daily basis: "You are not acceptable as you are; your likes and desires are not the right ones; you need to buy something you don't already have or become something you are not. In your current state you aren't enough—not happy enough, not productive enough, not safe enough, not sexy enough, etc." No matter what product a company is selling, we are told that we need it to fill a hole or fix a failing. Not only that, but because belonging is so essential to our well-being, we are primed to accept anything that promises to make us whole again and return us to the group.

This kind of socialization operates like polluted air: invisible and pervasive, affecting everyone who breathes it even if they take steps to protect themselves. It saturates us with anxiety, misplaced ambition, and insatiable longing. Attending to the constant demands of socialization, we lose the time and energy it takes to create a joyful life—one that feels satisfying and fulfilling to our unique, individual selves.

Because the "I'm not enough" idea is planted in us from a very early age, most of us have never questioned whether or not it's true. Everyone I know who manages to grow into a full, creative expression of life has embraced an opposite truth: *you are enough, perfect exactly as you are, right now.* This feels radical for most of us.

What if this truth is a seed that can grow within if you are willing to let it? As unfamiliar as it may feel for many of us as adults, it was certainly there when we were born, as no baby or very young child starts life with this idea. I invite you to plant the seed with this question: What if I were enough? The question primes the soil for transformation; just being open to it starts to allow space for you to imagine, to see yourself as who you are meant to be. Nurture the growth of this seedling truth, and watch as the roots and branches reach toward a deeper connection with your inner creative self.

Tools for Fostering Conscious Creativity

The good news is that socialization itself is an act of creativity—making imagination real. It's often unconscious, though, with negative and restrictive messaging passed down blindly through generations of cultural belief. By bringing conscious creativity to bear on socialization, we can imagine new ways of being that enrich our lives with bounteous joy, connection, and true belonging.

I'll have some exercises at the end of this chapter to help you strengthen your imagination muscles and spot instances of socialization, but in the meantime I'd like you to consider the tools below that have made their way around creative circles and that I often include when teaching my classes.

Setting Limits

It's a well-known paradox that certain kinds of limits can create the conditions to spark our imaginations. You can use this to your favor by creating limits for yourself. For instance, grab your journal and write a very brief (two- to three-paragraph) romance story. The limitation is that the female in the relationship is seventy-five and the male in the relationship is thirty-three. Or jot down a list of all the foods you would love to eat while respecting the limit of not using your teeth. You could go on a silent retreat where you don't speak at all (or create one for yourself for a day at home). Even setting a timer for two minutes for a serious or silly task can be a cool limitation. For example, you might say, "I'm going to give myself nonstop compliments for the next two minutes."

Shifting Your Perspective

Remember how the root of imagination is the act of seeing? Perspective taking can be fun or serious, but at its heart it simply involves changing how you see something. When you're making a decision at home or at work, it might mean agreeing to "switch" with someone who has a different point of view. As an exercise, you argue their case and they take yours. Or it can be a simple daydream, like spending a few minutes imagining that you've been shrunk to the size of a nickel. What does the world look like? Feel like? When you come back into your own size, how do you feel?

Welcoming Randomness

One of the simplest ways to unlock our natural capacity for imagination is to give ourselves some random input. This might be choosing a card from a deck or opening a book to a random page to provide inspiration. You can write a poem where each line starts with a word pulled from a hat. Or create a drawing with only three colors chosen from a box of markers with your eyes closed. Ask a child in your life to name any three foods, and then build a meal around them. Randomness takes the pressure out of feeling like you have to invent something out of thin air, allowing the imagination to respond in its natural way. I have included one of my favorite exercises around this concept at the end of this chapter, which uses randomness to creatively solve a problem.

Transforming Dread into Possibility

There's one way that our imagination is often still as powerful as it was when we were children, if not more so, and that's when it comes to painting images of what we fear. Most of us are quite adept at creating mental scenes of loss, risk, and limitation, even if we feel less imaginative when it comes to possibilities. Furthermore, some of us subscribe to the idea that if we can imagine the worst possible outcome to any situation, then we will somehow be better prepared to deal with it or "grateful" when it doesn't come to pass. We may even hold an inverted superstitious belief that we need to think about every possible bad outcome in an effort to prevent those very things from happening.

Meanwhile, back in reality, the vast majority of what we fear never actually occurs. I have a friend who likes to say, "Ninety-nine percent of my worst days never happened, except in my own mind." Yet the imagination is so powerful, in some ways the mind and body *do experience* these horrifying scenarios, flooding our body with stress hormones that wear down our health and happiness and disconnecting us from our joy.

Do you have this mental habit of projecting images of things you dread? Me too, though I've learned to keep a watchful eye on this habit so that it doesn't control me in the way it once did. As you start to gain mastery of your imagination, you may begin to notice how often you picture the worst in vivid detail. Many people do this from time to time, and it's nothing to be ashamed of. It's simply a mental muscle memory, like tying your shoes or driving all the way to work without ever thinking about how you do it.

When the imagination has been stunted or bent toward fear and anxiety, it becomes an internal enemy, a saboteur who works to keep you feeling stuck and small or even actively creates things you don't want. Your imagination is like a magnifying glass. You choose where to point it and what it illuminates and expands, whether that's scenes of fear and lack or stories of creativity and possibility.

The good news is that retraining your imagination muscle is easier than you think, and it almost immediately comes back online as a mentor and muse. No matter what happened to darken or dull your imagination, it is possible to heal it, to return it to its natural positive function. One seemingly counterintuitive way to do so is when you catch yourself envisioning the worst, choose to be bored instead.

The Unlikely Magic of Boredom

In our fast-paced, highly connected world, we often get the message that boredom is unwanted and unnecessary. Faced with a waiting room, traffic jam, or afternoon with nothing to do, most of us instinctively reach for our devices, a snack, or something "productive" to fill our time, as if boredom were a disease to be avoided at all costs. I know for sure, however, that a certain amount of boredom—and the ability to resist "fixing" it—has some surprising creative benefits.

When we're bored, our mind may wrestle with inactivity at first. Without something immediate we have to do, think about, or engage with, we're left with our feelings and sensations. Our thinking, ruminating mind—often thought of as the left brain—wants to explain these feelings, push away any discomfort, and get on with logical business or outside stimuli. The more creative, emotional part of our mind—the right brain—needs a certain amount of empty space and time to do its thing. In other words, if we're scrolling through images on social media, we literally don't have the capacity to come up with rich, rewarding mental images of our own.

Boredom doesn't always feel great in the moment. Much like meditation, we often don't feel the immediate benefit of sitting patiently with boredom while we're in the middle of it. The benefit comes later, as the mind learns to relax. Unexpected ideas, a sense of spaciousness, embracing calm, a shift in the perception of time, and increased focus and memory all come along when we give ourselves some room to breathe and be bored.

If you're operating in constant distraction or you always feel the need to be productive, it becomes almost impossible to grab hold of these benefits. In fact, you are likely to experience mental fatigue instead. Consider this for a moment: Have you ever given up on a problem out of frustration, taken a nap or a walk, and suddenly you get a flash of inspiration in the downtime? This is no accident—and you can build your capacity for more of these fertile moments.

It may seem ironic, but if you want to develop things like concentration, focus, and creativity, then I suggest building some time for boredom into your schedule. These empty pockets of time are like stretch, relaxation, and recovery periods for your mental muscles.

In my own journey of self-discovery, I've found that my constant need for distraction was tied to a lack of self-acceptance. Likewise, many of my clients who have trouble accepting boredom also suffer from a feeling of not being creative or interesting enough or not doing enough. This is another form of socialization at work. What about you? Is your desire to stay busy and engaged coming from genuine joy and excitement, or are you avoiding yourself in some way, thinking you should achieve some "better" version of yourself in the future?

Can you set these unhelpful ideas and behaviors aside, acknowledging that socialization can lead us away from our deepest creative impulses and shut down our imagination?

At least once a week, and hopefully more, I invite you schedule thirty minutes during which you will do absolutely nothing. Put away your smartphone and other devices. Hang a note on your office or bedroom door. This is not productive time. Let go of any voice telling you to read, write in your journal, or meditate. Ignore your to-do list. You're not looking for anything. You are doing nothing on purpose.

In your quiet, undisturbed spot, sit and do nothing. If something comes into your consciousness, that's fine. Accept it, then let it go. Sit and let your mind settle into a space where nothing is expected of you.

This sounds simple, but it can be very challenging for many of us. If you find yourself becoming agitated, remember to take some deep breaths. It might also help to say to yourself, "I am really agitated right now. I'm restless." Acknowledging your physical reaction to doing nothing can sometimes help to dispel your restlessness.

The point here is to just be. After some practice, you are likely to notice feelings or have small aha moments and inspirations, but don't make an effort to do more than notice them. You can recall them later and describe them in your journal if you need to, but during this time simply become an observer.

My experience is that boredom is vital to imagination, which marks the beginning of creativity and the return to your inner creative self. The exercises that follow can be adapted to suit your needs, but their main purpose is to create mental and emotional space for your imagination to develop and thrive in positive and healing ways.

Exercise: Problem-Solving with Random Words

This is an exercise to try when you're having trouble tuning in to your imagination. I find it especially valuable to bring some new insight into a problem or issue.

To start, call to mind an problem where you feel stuck. It might be a project at work or a conflict with a loved one. In your journal, briefly describe the problem.

Example: Constant conflict with my teen about homework.

Next, using an online random word generator—easily found through any search engine—grab the first word you find. Alternately, you can open a dictionary or another book to a random page and point with your eyes closed.

Example: Basket

Note: The random word does not provide solutions. Rather, think of it as a prompt that moves your thinking forward in a new way, providing anything but "right" answers. Now do some writing about the ways in which your problem, or any aspect of it, might be like this word. Our brains are incredible connection makers and storytellers. When one line of thinking peters out, keep going—just like the kindergarten kids and their chalk dot.

> *Example*: I am a basket case! This is making me crazy, the constant nagging and fighting. How is homework like a basket? Well, there's an in-basket at work, where everything gets collected, and then it has to be processed. That's one of the issues: he never seems to know how much he has to do until it's too late. A basket is also a container, but often with holes, or breathable. Maybe he can come up with a

container to do the work, but it can still be flexible and breathable. Like setting a timer for 20 minutes and seeing how much can get done in that time. He gets to choose the time and the area he works in. Baskets are also containers that can be filled and emptied, picked up and moved to new places. Maybe I can see this problem in that way, so that I don't have to think about it all the time and nag him. We can put little pieces of paper in a physical "homework" basket—stuff that's due, things he needs help with, etc.—and I can put a reminder in the calendar for a time we both agree to sit down and unpack the basket. Then I can let go of the constant nagging—every time I think of it I can drop my thought into the basket instead of yelling at him.

Going through this process turns your imagination on and allows new ideas to surface. You can even do this exercise with someone else. In this example, the teen might also have some interesting ideas to solve the problem in a new way.

Exercise: Daydreaming Meditation

For this practice, find a comfortable seat in a quiet spot where you can be undisturbed for up to ten minutes.

When you are settled in, set a timer on your phone for five minutes. That way you don't have to be concerned with how long you are doing this practice. When the timer goes off, you're done.

Begin by breathing deeply and doing a body scan, looking for any areas that feel tight or uncomfortable, where you might be hiding stress or anxiety. Imagine that you are gathering all of the stress and anxiety from wherever it's hiding in your body. Breathe it out and see it leaving your mouth like a cloud of dark smoke, dissipating and floating away from you.

Once you've done this three or four times, let your eyes go soft and imagine someone you really love. This could be a friend or family member, someone you see regularly, or someone you haven't seen in years, from childhood or adulthood.

Now you and this person you love are going on a journey together. You can go anywhere in the world—or beyond the world, if you prefer. Where are you two going? What will you be doing there? Who will you meet? What conversations will you have? Be specific.

The only rule for this exercise is that you focus your imagination on something that feels wonderful. If you notice your mind bringing up something dark or painful, which often happens at first, you can gently say to yourself, "That's okay. We'll get to that soon. But for right now, we're doing something we love . . ."

You may feel like you're breaking the rules or you might experience a lot of anxiety when you try this at first. That's natural. You're likely hearing old, critical voices telling you to "grow up and stop daydreaming." Or maybe you hear, "You're wasting time. Get back to work." Remember that your imagination is your own private realm. Even in a day full of pressure and deadlines, you can take a short break and give yourself total freedom to explore an inner journey to anywhere you want to go.

I've noticed that when my students do this easy meditation, they report a sense of timelessness and expansiveness. Five minutes of on-purpose daydreaming sometimes feel like hours. This practice of positive imagining activates happy chemicals in our brains, so even the briefest of mental vacations can send us back to our heavy-duty adult day feeling much lighter and freer.

Exercise: Artist Dates

Many of us feel obligated to fill every moment with useful, practical things and forget that by giving the inner self room to breathe, feel, and express itself, we recharge our batteries in a profound way.

Even if you are a creative professional, it's good to set aside time for projects that you do for the pure joy of it, without the pressure associated with performance. Many notable creatives do exactly this.

Julia Cameron prescribes what she calls *artist dates* in her book *The Artist's Way*. These regular, solitary appointments take us out of our ordinary experience, nourishing the spirit and reviving the senses. Julia called me one night, and as we spoke, she described her artist date from earlier that evening:

> I went to the bookstore and sat in the children's section and read part of *Black Beauty*. It was a book I loved as a young girl, and I've had trouble reading bigger books lately. Reading in that little chair surrounded by other children's books reminded me how it's meant to feel.

I recommend making (and keeping!) a regular artist date with yourself, at least once or twice a month. Set aside a couple of hours of undisturbed time. Write it in your calendar and let the people around you know that it's important to you.

In your journal, jot down a few notes for what you'd like to do on your next artist date. Feel free to plan something seemingly childish or unimportant. I only ask that it's something that brings you joy, a change in perspective, a chance to reflect and relax, or all of the above. The result is often a renewed imagination and creative outlook.

Next . . . go do it!

Exercise: Shoulds and Shouldn'ts— the Tools of Socialization

I'd like you to start paying attention to how often you say, hear, or think these words: "I should . . ." or "I shouldn't . . ."

I should be further along in my career.

I should be in a relationship/have a better relationship.

I should be skinnier/in better shape.

I should feel grateful for _____ and be happy about it.

I shouldn't feel the way I do about this situation.

I shouldn't do _____ at my age.

Should and *shouldn't* are two little words that can be powerhouse tools of socialization—others use them on us, and we use them on ourselves. When we say these loaded words to ourselves, they often carry an implicit judgment along the lines of, *I'm not doing the right thing. I'm not doing enough. I need to be better, I need to be different, I need to think or feel differently*, and so on.

For now, it's enough to simply notice these words and begin asking whether or not whatever is being suggested feels right to you. Check in with your body and see if you sense a tightness in your chest or throat with these statements or if you feel an expansion and opening.

In other words, do you feel an inner "yes" or "no"? For example, *Yes! I should be further in my career, so it's time to stop making excuses.* Or, *No, I'm judging myself by someone else's standard, and I'm going to choose what brings me joy as my path to success.*

Use this practice to gradually build a curiosity habit, so that every time you hear yourself say or think *I should/shouldn't,* you can pause and ask, *Is this really true for me? Or is this socialization at work?*

Keep this list handy, as we will return to it later on.

Exercise: What If You Are Perfect Now?

As I mentioned earlier, many of us have been socialized to the idea that we are somehow "not enough"—not tall enough, short enough, smart enough, sexy enough. This can lead us to struggle with our own self-worth and think that in order to change anything we'll have to be harder on ourselves or do something difficult or painful. Imagine the proverbial drill sergeant in your mind, pushing you to be something better than you are right now. This exercise reminds us that warm, loving energy can create more effective and long-lasting change.

Creativity is the act of turning imagination into reality, so it follows that two of the most powerful creative words are "What if . . ."

We will explore the infinite possibility of these words over the course of this book, but for now I want you to write in your journal:

What if I am perfect just as I am right now?

What if I am enough?

What if everything is just as it should be right this moment?

What if I am doing the best I can?

You don't have to answer these questions necessarily; just ask them, consider them, and feel whatever emotions they bring up for you. Think about what things would look like and feel like to you if these statements were all true. Of course, you may feel moved to write the answers in your journal, and I encourage you to do so.

These questions set the stage for reconnecting to your inner creative self, making space for imagination to combine with self-discovery practices like the exercises in this book, which I encourage you to return to again and again. Remember, this is a process. You don't have to wait until you are healed to be creative; rather, you practice creativity in ways that nurture your healing.

Four

Rediscovering Intuition and Honoring Emotions

Intuition is the key to everything, in painting, film-making, business—everything. I think you could have an intellectual ability, but if you can sharpen your intuition . . . a knowingness occurs.
—David Lynch

A friend of mine once found herself in a seemingly hopeless financial situation, exhausted and emotionally drained by her career and not able to see any way out. One night, she got a random "hit" of intuition. Out of the blue, she felt sure she must go through and organize her whole apartment. She had no idea why—this organization didn't seem to have any relationship to her long-term hopes and dreams, much less her immediate financial need. Still, she has a strong relationship with her intuition, so even though she didn't feel like she had extra time to do this task, she made a commitment to do so.

Using clutter clearing expert Marie Kondo's principle of keeping only the things that "spark joy" and discarding the rest, over the course of the next couple of weeks she went through everything she owned. The process was difficult in some moments, gratifying in others, but always led by joy. As she went, she began to notice that everyday activities that had felt mundane or depressing before—entering a cluttered bedroom, cooking a meal, or taking a shower—suddenly became delightful simply because she'd made conscious choices about what to keep and what to discard, and she loved everything that was left.

Finally, after a busy two weeks, she wrapped up the process. I kid you not, *the following day* she got a phone call with a job offer in a city she had long dreamed of living in. It was Thursday, and she'd have to report on Monday. Could she do it? Yes. In fact, she was ready to go, in every possible way. Everything in her space was ready to be put into moving boxes and shipped to a place where new opportunity awaited.

My friend could have easily dismissed her intuition. After all, logical thinking would struggle to make any connection between organizing an apartment and receiving a life-changing job offer. Yet I imagine that you've had a few similar experiences yourself, times when you listened to your gut feelings (or wish you had) and it changed your life.

What is this mysterious force we call intuition? Merriam-Webster defines it as "a thing that one knows or considers likely from *instinctive feeling* rather than conscious reasoning." In other words, this kind of knowing often doesn't make logical sense; it comes from someplace else.

For many of those who have claimed the title artist, like filmmaker David Lynch, whose quote begins this chapter, the connection between creativity and intuition is undeniable. Other writers and artists have even described an almost trancelike state while they are immersed in creative practice, where they feel a vital connection to their intuition. During these times, the person will often experience time in a different way, with hours seeming to pass in minutes, and creative ideas or images may arise that defy logical understanding in the moment but become meaningful in profound ways later on. Others have called this state "flow." Whatever you call it, intuition and creativity thrive when they work in conjunction with one another.

Knowing Before Knowing

I also believe that our intuition can help us make decisions or take actions based on an intelligence that sometimes we aren't even aware of at the time.

For example, a friend of mine went on a camping trip as a young teenager and at one point had a race with his friends down a mountain and back to their campsite. At the end of the trail, there was a barrier about three feet high. My friend was in the lead, excited and having a blast, and instead of stopping to climb over the barrier, as he normally would have, he leaped from several feet back, just clearing it.

He turned around to gloat about his win, and all his friends were standing well back from the barrier, eyes wide in fear. As they gently edged around to either side of the barrier, he looked down and saw the angry rattlesnake he'd leaped over moments before.

My friend made a life-altering decision without the benefit of any noticeable nudge from his intuition, but does that mean it was just dumb luck? Perhaps. But I don't think so (my intuition tells me otherwise!), and it turns out there is some scientific evidence that supports this as well.

Author and neuropsychologist Chris Niebauer explains how recent studies have shown that the right brain, long thought to be the place where creativity resides, can evaluate situations and lead us to take actions that are in our own best interest before we ever make a left brain, logic-based, or rational decision.

In one study he cites in his book, *No Self, No Problem*, subjects in a gaming experiment were able to detect patterns in two decks of cards that would lead to more wins or losses, and their heart rate increased and sweat glands opened when they reached for the "risky" deck. This nervous reaction to the "risky" deck occurred before their conscious mind had realized the same pattern, *so subjects couldn't explain why they felt the way they did.*

Have you ever made a decision without giving it much thought and then later found out that it was life-altering? Just like my friend's quick jump, I believe that our intuition is working on our behalf even when we aren't conscious of it. Just imagine how powerful it can be when we work with it consciously.

For these reasons, I see intuition as a kind of untapped superpower. It informs not only my artistic and creative pursuits, but my whole life. I would no more do without it today than I would food or water. I rely on it for everything, from minor choices like which direction to drive home to much larger decisions such as relocating across the country or choosing a romantic partner. Looking back, I can see now that when I began to listen to and follow my intuition, that was when I really began to feel like the artist of my own life.

The problem is that most of us weren't taught the skill of listening to and following our intuition, as we live in a society that's imbued with a logic-based cultural bias. This makes us wary to trust our gut feelings or notice the kinds of irregular patterns or even weird events that the right brain excels at processing. The logic-based left brain wants to make our perceptions fit through the keyhole of what we already know. If you go back and read that last sentence, you will see that it's the opposite of creativity, which by definition leads us into the unknown.

I can't imagine returning to a time when I shut down the guidance of that interior voice. When we shut down or ignore our intuition, as so many of us have been trained to do, it's no surprise that the element of joy in our life suffers. To be clear, I'm not suggesting that our intuition replace logical thinking, but rather that we want to bring more balance to our lives by using both aspects. In other words, we owe it to ourselves to use logic and critical thinking *and* listen to and follow our intuition. In my experience, pursuing this harmony unleashes an astonishing creative force in all areas of our lives. When we open ourselves to our own inner knowing, we turn on antennae that send and receive information beyond the limits of the rational mind. We are able to absorb messages that are not available to us if we always stay within the normal perceptions. Insights, moments of clarity, and epiphanies find their way through and can inform daily life when we learn how to cultivate this native state. This is the inner creative self in action.

If you feel you've lost touch with your intuition, reconnecting to it can feel awkward at first. You may not feel confident in distinguishing between an intuitive feeling and wishful thinking. You might fall into old habits, fears, or biases and think that they are protective warnings. Like any other skill, it takes a willingness to keep trying—trusting and experimenting, paying attention to how things play out, and checking in with your feelings again and again. I'll have an exercise at the end of this chapter to help you fine-tune your own intuitive connection. In the meantime, here are a couple of creative ideas to help reconnect you to your intuition.

Blind Contour Drawing

This is a great exercise to take you out of your logical, results-oriented mind and into the realm of pure observation and creative flow. Contour drawing means drawing the outline of an item, such as a hand. Blind contour drawing entails trying to draw that same hand without ever looking at your paper or lifting your pencil up. No erasing, no stopping and reviewing, just pure drawing based on observation. The results may look a little wild, but allow for this crazy imperfection to be what it is without the need to erase or change it.

Keeping a Dream Log

Our dreaming life operates on a symbolic, metaphorical level. Many cultures throughout human history have taught that we can learn about ourselves and our intuition by paying attention to our dreams and seeing what symbols, events, and people we find there. One way to begin to explore this rich, symbolic world is to keep a log or journal of your dreams. This can be in your regular journal you've been working with so far, or it can be a special dream journal just for this purpose. The trick is to keep it next to your bed, and every morning as soon as you wake up (this is key, as we forget most of our dreams as the day goes on), jot down some notes about what you remember from your dreams the night before. If you can't recall your dreams, jot down even the smallest fragment you can remember, or just write "I don't remember my dreams from last night, but I'm sure I will tomorrow." This sends a signal to your unconscious mind that you are paying attention and would like to remember your dreams going forward.

With patience, many people find that writing about their dreams in this way can help them recall them with finer and finer detail. Once you've recorded a few days' worth of dreams, go back and review what you've written. Ask your intuition what a particular dream might mean and how you might act on this new information.

Intuitive Painting

It's easy to get bogged down in the compulsion to paint as realistically as possible, but abstract painting has a rich history and can be an amazing tool for developing and honoring your intuition. Grab some paints (acrylics and watercolor are both relatively cheap and easy to clean up), some paper or canvas, and start painting! Don't think about it as you do so, just start putting paint on the canvas and see what arises. You can also play some music you like and put down color according to the rhythm of the music. Ask yourself if there's a color you especially want to look at in the moment— or perhaps there's already a color on the canvas that is "asking" to have a specific color next to it.

To take this to the next level, paint blindfolded, or do all of the above with finger paints. Let go of any expectations. You might be surprised at what appears in front of you!

Cultivating your intuition is a lifelong process best approached with curiosity, imagination, and even playfulness. What do you have to lose? You won't ever forget how to use the tools of reasoning or logical thinking. Let yourself ask the imaginative question, *What if . . . ?* In my experience, when you develop your intuition, creative solutions to life's challenges begin to appear—solutions that feel true and original because they are coming from your deepest desires that always nudge you toward your joy.

A Spectrum of Feelings

Another way to foster connection to your intuition and creativity is through learning to tune in to and trust your feelings and emotions. For many people, this can be another skill that's sorely out of practice, given that we live in a world that tends to value logical reasoning above all else. For example, you've likely received plenty of messages over the years about keeping your emotions in check. Take a look at this list of statements and see if any sound familiar to you:

Don't be a crybaby.

Keep a stiff upper lip.

Don't be at the mercy of your emotions.

You feel too much.

Don't be so sensitive.

You have to have a thick skin to make it in this world.

You're too emotional.

We've made some strides as a society when it comes to acknowledging that showing emotions is not a sign of weakness, but many of us still grapple with our culture's ingrained assumptions about our emotions. We simply don't know how to engage with them in a healthy way. This is how socialization leads us to favor logic over emotion, to discount the breadth and power of feelings, and to stay in the dark about what we're feeling most of the time.

The good news is that working with our emotions can be one of our most helpful tools in healing the connection to our inner creative self, reactivating our intuition, and leading us to our heart's true joy. Honoring emotions allows our creative expression to manifest in a multitude of ways. On the flip side, when we stuff our feelings down or reject their wisdom, they can transform into saboteurs, stagnating our creative process, reinforcing unhelpful behaviors, and sapping our imaginative power.

We often don't express in words the broad range of human emotions and tend to reduce what we feel to only a few—happy, sad, angry. In fact, there are tens of thousands of distinct feelings. Your own range of authentic feelings is like a personal color palette that offers tremendous opportunity for expression in many forms. Emotions infuse the pictures in your imagination with energy—and can make them feel as real in your body as when the events happen in reality.

Imagine walking into a wine cellar with thousands of bottles displayed in the racks, tasting a couple, and then saying, "It's all just wine to me." To a wine connoisseur, this place is filled with treasure. Each bottle has its own combination of special attributes. Some are more robust, earthy, or buttery. These bottles are alive with stories of sunny hillsides, rainstorms, and frost. People touched the grapes with their hands and poured love into these bottles.

We can become connoisseurs of emotion by giving our feelings the unique attention they deserve. When we attend to emotions in this way, we activate cues in our imagination, which can expand into all areas of our lives. Knowing that we are feeling specific feelings like daring, pensive, helpless, or serene grants us permission to go deep into the experience—both current and imagined. Every feeling we experience is a shade of paint that we can use to express our creative inner selves.

Feelings and emotions can also be a helpful guidance system when making better decisions, but we are mostly taught to downplay or disregard them, to rely on the logical mind and remain unclouded by emotional bias.

But you can't think your way out of a feeling.

In fact, as neuroscientist Jill Bolte Taylor tells us, "Although many of us think of ourselves as thinking creatures that feel, biologically we are feeling creatures that think." The evolution of the feeling part of our brain predates the thinking part by tens of thousands of years.

Our feelings aren't 100 percent right about everything, though; our logic must also play an important role in our decision-making and creative processes. So how can these tools dance together? We can start by honoring both, and understanding that feelings are guides that always tell *a* truth, even if it's not the ultimate truth about the present situation.

Many of us struggle to find this balance and trust our emotions and intuition due in part to the lasting influence of one of the enemies of creativity: trauma.

Traumatic Experiences

One night in my mid-twenties, I settled in to watch the movie *Good Will Hunting*, in which Matt Damon stars as Will Hunting, a poor, tough street kid with a genius IQ. As Will went through the excruciating process of court-ordered therapy, something broke open in me. His therapist, played by Robin Williams, wrapped his arms around Will and said over and over, "It's not your fault. It's not your fault."

By the time the credits rolled, I was sobbing. As I stood, I stumbled and wondered why the film had shaken me so deeply. I also felt shame about equating my own story with that of this severely abused kid in the movie. How dare I pretend that my experiences were anything like his? I didn't have any scars from cigarette burns or stabs on my body like he did. I hadn't bounced around a series of terrible foster homes. I dried my face and stuffed whatever had just happened back inside, "where it belonged." It would not be until many years later that I reopened this locked cell and began the process of inviting my own trauma into the light.

I share this story because it points to a common misunderstanding about trauma, namely that only extreme events qualify as traumatic. No one would doubt that events such as assault or abuse are traumatic, but many other experiences that get downplayed as "not that bad" also have an intense effect on our psyche. Furthermore, an event that does not unfold as trauma for one person might be traumatic for someone else—everything from personal history to neurobiology is at play here.

The death of a loved one, divorce, illness, financial setback, job loss, physical accident, and the like can all be traumatic. Many of us deal with systemic traumas, like those perpetuated on communities of color, people who are poor, and other groups that are marginalized or victimized. Trauma can arise from social hurts, such as being bullied or excluded, or any other type of humiliating experience that occurred during our formative years. In any form, trauma changes our behavior, affects our beliefs about ourselves and our potential, and degrades our long-term well-being.

Trauma of any kind often hijacks our emotions and distorts our relationship to them, and we often leave them unexpressed. The problem is that unexpressed emotions don't just go away; they can linger and settle in the body, preventing us from living the life we desire and sometimes even causing physical pain or disease. Depending on the cause, trauma may make it harder to trust ourselves and others, cause us to doubt our abilities, or even saddle us with incredible guilt and resentment. All of these close us off to our joy and sever our connection to our inner creative self.

Healing from trauma is also healing the connection to your inner creative self, which often involves giving your feelings expression in the outer world. You don't have to share all your feelings all the time. You can always commit to exploring them for yourself and then share them with others when it's necessary for you. A great place to start doing this is in your journal practice, and I've included an exercise at the end of this chapter to help.

When it comes to trauma, it's not really about what specifically happened—it's about the impact that your experiences have on you and how you change your behavior or otherwise develop survival strategies to function as a result. Noted psychologist Nicole LePera teaches that childhood traumatic experiences can be subtle. When a child doesn't feel seen or heard or when a parent manipulates, controls, or lives vicariously through a child, those experiences can be traumatic, and that's exactly the type of trauma that can lead to long-term disconnection from the inner creative self.

The effects of unhealed trauma might include anxiety disorders, depression, eating disorders, addiction, people-pleasing behavior, and more. Each of these depletes our well-being, as the inner creative self is giving away some of its power and freedom to the demands of a condition or behavior. If you are willing to do the inner work of seeing and feeling the troubled, tender spots that grow from trauma, you reclaim the vitality of your inner creative self.

Think of the revitalizing power of the sun soaking into the leaves of a wilted plant. We can bring traumatic experiences into the light in this way, by acknowledging what occurred and how it still affects our behavior and outlook. This isn't about wallowing in past hurts or being a victim—rather, the idea is to unfurl into the sunshine, absorbing the healing. If we keep trauma buried or secret, we may feel we're protecting ourselves, but we're actually cutting off access to the healing power of light and truth.

This deep work of looking within isn't easy, but it frees us from our internal bondage to the past and opens us up to feeling our joy. This is a kind of seesaw process: as you acknowledge and heal these wounds, it may bring forward more pain for the moment, but you'll also experience the joy and calm of returning to your inner creative self. This in turn sets off more self-exploration, which fortifies your creative spirit even further. This expanding relationship to your deepest self becomes the journey that is in fact your long-awaited destination.

I believe that we are safest, most joyful, and most energized in life when we honor our emotions and listen to our intuition. The combination of emotion and intuition may be best described by the phrase "trust your gut." And doing exactly that is what frees your inner creative self.

Because every person is unique, the way we receive messages from our intuition will be unique too. Some of us literally have a gut feeling, such as butterflies in the stomach, while others may have a picture or a thought flash through their mind when considering a decision. Others will have their attention brought to something outside themselves; perhaps an animal, photo, or other object presents itself in a meaningful way. I've even heard of people who experience a certain smell that they know from past experience is their intuition.

Thinking back, are there times your intuition spoke to you? Did it happen in one of these ways? Make a list of anything you remember in your journal. Don't worry if you can't think of any examples right now. You'll be building up your intuition regardless. Now let's look at some specific ways of how you can do so.

Using Your Intuition for Small Decisions

One way to strengthen your intuition and get in a habit of using it is to listen to its input about small decisions you make throughout your day.

For example, if you need to go to the grocery store, then the library, then the dry cleaners, take a moment as you head out the door to ask, *Which one first?* Whatever the answer or sensation points you to, follow it. Even if it's not the most "logical" way to organize your errands, go with whatever gut feeling or other intuitive nudge that guides you.

Make a note in your journal of how you received the intuitive guidance. If something happens later that seems to justify your intuition (for example, you found out that there was a traffic jam on the way to the grocery store that cleared up just as you left the library), make a note of that as well. But don't feel disappointed if nothing happens to confirm your intuition. Either way, this exercise trains you to notice when your intuition is speaking and to follow its guidance.

Intuition and Big Decisions

Here's a practice for when you're facing a big decision, a complex situation, or a problem you've been wrestling with for a long time. This practice can be especially useful if you've done a lot of "logical" work on the issue already and you've tried to figure it out and do something about it in every way you know how.

On a notepad or in your journal, write one sentence that describes the issue or even a single word. Notice where you feel the thing in your body, and take a moment to name the emotions it brings up as specifically as you can. Also notice if your mind wants to say, "this is silly," or explain away that feeling in your body. If this happens, you can quietly remind yourself that there will be plenty of time for rational thinking, but for now you are opening yourself up to your intuitive right brain.

Next, let go of the details of the situation. Pretend that you are looking at a picture and you've relaxed your eyes, allowing things get a little bit fuzzy. You aren't focused on any one thing, and you can take in the bigger picture in a more sensory way. You're not looking for conclusions or solutions, just noticing the landscape. From this perspective, spend a little time in your imagination and think about these words: *What would bring me joy in this situation?*

Let yourself create a picture of an end result you would love, and sit with this image for a moment. Feel the emotions that come up as you experience this ideal outcome, where your issue has been solved in a way that brings you joy. Write down in your journal what this looks like, without editing yourself. Don't be concerned with anything being realistic or even plausible right now. Your focus is on what would bring you joy in the situation, no matter where that leads you.

As you wrap up this portion of the exercise, write in your journal and say aloud, "Let it be so."

Even the most impossible situations have the potential to unfold in a way that will bring you joy or you would love. You can *feel* it by doing this exercise, which lays the groundwork for imagination to become reality. Now, as you go through the days ahead, be on the lookout for messages from your intuition that may show you actions to take that will move you toward your desired outcome. Look out for any synchronistic events, clues, or other information that shows up. It's not important that they all make sense right away; if you are patient, you will begin to get the feeling that you've activated a mysterious domino effect. You are experiencing your deeper creative nature as it seeks to produce the result you desire. After all, your inner creative nature is part of the greater nature of life, and life always finds a way.

The next best step—and it may be a tiny one—will appear, but it will likely not be what you think it should be. Remember, the *feeling* of the desired result is what you really want in the end. I have found that while the situation might not resolve itself in the exact way you imagined, it may very well do so in a way that brings you joy, and that is ultimately what you're really after.

Daily Feeling Check-In

Many of us don't have a practice of checking in on our emotions. My hope is that you will begin one, as doing so is a consistent way to bring balance between your logical side and your feeling side, and you'll be more acquainted with spotting, identifying, and sharing emotions when they come up for more serious events, rather than ignoring them or pushing them down. One easy way to do this is to simply check in with yourself once a day and find out how you're feeling.

For simplicity's sake, I suggest doing this at noon every day or as soon after noon as works in your schedule. You may want to set a reminder on your phone until it becomes a habit. Try not to justify, excuse, or minimize your feelings. Just notice them and be as specific as you can in naming them. This is simple but can be profound in that you begin to notice more emotions happening within you.

To do your check-in, take a moment to quiet yourself wherever you are and ask, *How am I feeling right now?* Is there anything that's bothering you? Is there something that is bringing you joy? And remember, there can be both. One of the amazing things about being human is that we can have multiple, sometimes even conflicting, emotions at the same time. Here is one of my recent check-ins that shows this quite well:

> I am feeling sad, lonely, and unworthy because of a recent breakup.

> I am also feeling grateful, empowered, and relieved because I know it was the right thing for us both at this time.

Try committing to this practice every day for fourteen days to start. You may find that at the end of that trial period you want to keep going.

Exercise: Naming Your Emotions

This practice can help you get more familiar with the vast array of emotions that are your creative fuel.

We feel comfortable with the idea that artists or performers express their emotions, whether that's as shades of paint on canvas, words that penetrate the soul, sounds that vibrate in your heart, or some other way. You can learn to display this mastery yourself, with your entire life as your artistic medium. When you tune in to the signals that come from within, learning their subtle differences and expressing them with greater accuracy, you find that emotions are an infinite wellspring of creativity.

Let's try this now with the help of your journal. As a reminder, you can do this practice at any point in your day, whether you have a moment to write it down or not.

To begin, have your journal and pen nearby, and then relax and pause your body for two or three minutes. Focus on your breath: the in and out, the rise and the fall of your chest and belly, the flow of air into and out of your nose. Let your body settle.

Now ask yourself, *How am I feeling right now?* Then write down one word to describe how you are feeling. Perhaps that word is *calm*, or *anxious*, or *sad*, or *happy*.

That's your start. You may think of more than one word for what you're feeling, and that's wonderful. For now, stick with one, and you can always continue this exercise with any other words that come up for you. Human emotion is complex and often contradictory.

Now let's go a little deeper. Close your eyes and do a scan of your body. Where do you feel this emotion in your body? Notice the actual sensations—give them a color, shape, temperature, and texture. Do you feel warmth, tightness, heaviness, etc.?

At this point, a word may come to you that gets even closer to whatever it is you're feeling. Once you've felt the softening of your chest and a nice fullness in your belly, your initial *happy* feeling might become *peaceful* or *satisfied*. If you notice a jittery feeling in your legs, you might identify your emotion as *anxious* or *jumpy*. For now, try to stay with the feeling itself and its associated physical sensations, rather than a story about the feelings.

If these more specific words come to you, write them in your journal. You can also draw or sketch your feelings. Another option is to stand and move your body to express a particular feeling.

Next, see if you can describe the mental story that's driving your feelings. Your anxiety might be related to a big project that's due at work this week, your to-do list around the house, or perhaps just a general feeling of overwhelm. Honor the story and the emotions that come with it. You might even speak to yourself in a calming way, saying something like, *It's so hard to feel like there's more to do than you can possibly manage.* Remember, the feeling tells a truth that can help us.

This nervousness can be productive if you listen to it and don't try to shove it away. For example, you might write, "It looks like I need to renegotiate some of my commitments at work and home, so that I can be excited about what I have to get done and can tackle it piece by piece."

This practice has the power to draw you into a more creative expression of what you're feeling, unearthing the mental story that is contributing to the feeling and then offering a rewrite of the story if it's not a feeling you want to keep. For those feelings that you'd like to foster more in your life, the best thing to do is to lean into them and allow yourself to experience them fully. In this way, you are training your inner creative self to relish and take time to feel positive emotions.

Doing this practice regularly helps you know yourself at a deeper level and exercise your creativity simultaneously.

Five

Reclaiming the Power of Story

The Universe is made of stories, not of atoms.
—Muriel Rukeyser

The Maori people of New Zealand have a myth of creation that is told through many different stories, all sharing the idea that at first there existed only nothingness, which transformed into darkness, and then into somethingness, or light. In his work *Metamorphoses*, the ancient Roman poet Ovid began his epic story of humanity by speaking of the initial chaos of the universe, containing in its formlessness all that was to become—elements, sky, living creatures. These and many other cultural creation stories mirror our current scientific theory of the big bang. Form from formlessness, light from darkness. It seems impossible that humans all over the world would have told stories and articulated metaphors to describe events that happened millennia before humanity ever arrived on the scene. Yet they have.

Maybe the universe is made of stories after all.

One thing is sure: for as long as humans have been on this earth, storytelling has formed an intrinsic pillar of our experience. This isn't surprising when you consider how the human mind is a storytelling apparatus. With the same regularity as the lungs breathe air and the heart pumps blood, the mind creates stories about what we perceive. To be human is to be creative. We all have a story-making mind, and in this way every single one of us is a storyteller.

Nowhere is this story-making more evident than in the story we tell ourselves about who we are. Of course, in many cases we will tell these stories about ourselves unconsciously, and as I've indicated already, that can be problematic. Unconscious stories are the ones formed in part by the forces of socialization, rejection, and traumatic experiences.

When we understand the mind's habit to tell stories, we can also choose to bring conscious awareness to them. Doing so makes us the authors or artists of our own stories, and this opens up whole new avenues of curiosity and self-knowledge and empowers us to discard or change any stories that aren't true for us. We get to rewrite, edit, or alter our story through the power of our creative nature.

What makes a good story? I would say the ingredients include the characters, the conflicts, and the journeys or quests, both small and large, that we undertake throughout our lives. Within this very basic framework lies infinite potential to create any kind of narrative, from a fun and silly bedtime story to a deeply personal conception of the meaning of one's own life.

We create these stories in collaboration with the people and cultures around us. For instance, our first story of who we are, our "character," is mostly based on what others tell us about ourselves as children and throughout life: "You're like this. You're good at this but not at that. In this family we do things this way." Whether through words or examples, the innocent child in us picks up these endless stories and incorporates them into our personal story.

I have a friend who has told me on several occasions, "My grandma used to say, 'Steve, you're an inch deep and a mile wide.' And she was right. I can talk a little bit about everything, but I've never really mastered anything." He repeats this as if it were a dictum carved into the stones of the Temple of Apollo. This observation informs my friend's identity, sets up certain internal and external conflicts, and frames the narrative of many of his relationships and personal challenges. I've always wondered if it's what he really wants for himself and why he seems to believe it without question.

That is a fairly benign example, too. I can't imagine that Steve's grandma was trying to hurt him. She probably said it half laughing at the time. Many such stories are more toxic, though.

How many times did you hear—or infer from society—things like these?

You can't do that. You're an idiot. You're unattractive. You're such a liar. You're just not creative. Your art is no good. You need to behave. You don't belong here. You can't sing. You make me so tired. You're too much. You need to play it safe.

Now think of how many times you've told *yourself* very similar things. Stories about who we are can become so ingrained in us that we no longer recognize them as stories. We mistake them for facts.

Psychology tells us that remaining consistent within our identity—who we believe ourselves to be— is one of the most powerful forces in the psyche. We will fight like hell to remain true to what we believe about ourselves, even if it contributes to a self-image that doesn't bring us joy.

We feel, think, and act from a litany of character traits that have been reinforced for so long they've become a subconscious part of our identity. In other words, we wouldn't *consciously* want to be some of these things; we don't *want* them to be the true stories of our lives, but deep within our psyches we've adopted these stories as concrete, irrefutable facts.

The resulting self-image, including the negative aspects we don't want, often lies below the surface of our conscious minds. As a result, when we behave in ways that confuse or disappoint our conscious standards, we find ourselves saying things like, *Why did I just do that . . . again?* The famous psychoanalyst Carl Jung referred to this as the shadow.

If a deep part of your mind believes you are undeserving, unworthy, uncreative, or anything like this, it pushes you into self-limiting behavior that is consistent with that belief. These things often baffle us, since we know deep down we don't want to do things that will lead us away from our greatest potential or bring us anything but joy.

Reconnecting consciously with your inner creative self allows you to play with and explore any element of your story at any time, gaining insights into how you really want to live, who you really are, and what brings real joy to your life. Rewriting your story is a profound creative practice that holds the potential for truly transformative healing. Later in this chapter, we'll look at some concrete ways to tap into your inner creative self and rewrite your story.

Before we do that, let's look again at how the first two enemies of creativity, socialization and traumatic experiences, can impact the stories we create about ourselves and our role in the world. Socialization is largely responsible for the first story of ourselves, as we base our opinion of who we are and what we like/dislike on what others tell us. Traumatic experiences have a huge impact on our stories too, often shaping them in ways we don't want. They often lead us to see the narrative of our past, present, and future through distorted or damaged lenses.

The third enemy of creativity, rejection, sits between socialization and traumatic experiences as a kind of conjoined triplet. Socialization uses the fear of rejection as a key instrument of discipline to keep us in line, and rejection can be traumatic in its own right. So while rejection is often related to the other two enemies of creativity, it has a personality all its own, one that is tied to our desire for perfection.

Rejection and Perfectionism

Take a moment and think back to your early school days and imagine this scenario with me: You are in class and the teacher asks a question, calls on you, and you declare the right answer. Feels pretty good, right? Now think about a scenario in which you get called on but get the wrong answer, and everyone in class laughs.

A simple example for sure, but can you imagine the negative emotions you might feel as a result of this simple form of rejection? Now consider the impact in instances when the rejection wasn't so benign—in an intimate relationship or close friendship, for example, or when you find out you didn't get a coveted job, promotion, or other goal you had aspired toward. That doesn't mean the rejections held nefarious intent, of course. It just means that you were experiencing the pain of not getting your heart's desire.

If these rejections happened at a young age and we weren't given the tools to deal with them in a healthy way, this can give support to the common belief we discussed earlier in the chapter on socialization, the one that says "I'm not enough." Anytime you tell this to yourself, it's the ultimate self-rejection. Seen in this light, I believe that the most tragic outcome of the rejection accrued over a lifetime of experiences is that we learn to reject ourselves.

The truth is that many of us weren't taught how to understand rejection in a healthy way, as "I am not enough" is one of the most prevalent beliefs in the human psyche, it's enforced by socialization and traumatic experiences, and for many it operates far below the surface of rational thought.

One way that rejection manifests is through the pursuit of perfectionism. Many people consider themselves to be perfectionists but don't realize that this desire is actually rooted in a fear of rejection. Perfectionism is especially acute when it comes to being creative and trying new things, as many otherwise confident people are rigid or afraid to try something new. The fear of rejection is so powerful that many people will decline to try something new without even realizing why.

Researcher Brené Brown goes even further and refers to perfectionism as "a self-destructive and addictive belief system that fuels this primary thought: 'If I look perfect, and do everything perfectly, I can avoid or minimize the painful feelings of shame, judgment, and blame.'"

In my experience, perfectionism is like a creative poison so many of us willingly drink, without realizing that it's paralyzing our ability to move toward our dreams and joy. We all carry the fear of rejection. We believe if we show up as our true self—inarticulate, awkward, still a work in progress—"they" will definitely throw us out.

Being creative requires diving into the unknown. What we don't know, we can't get perfectly right. So perfectionism keeps us on a tight leash, unwilling to let us expose ourselves to rejection. Children, of course, are still learning all the rules of life, and they have an expansive natural creative capacity. If they are raised in an open and encouraging environment, they are often not worried about doing something perfectly.

Unfortunately, many kids grow up in situations where they are expected to behave perfectly or face rejection, and the impressions left on them don't go away on their own once they reach adulthood. As a child, I almost never felt free of the expectation of perfection and the fear of rejection. As an adult, it was even worse. By the time I attended the life-changing retreat to which I referred in the introduction, I was wound so tightly—treading so carefully lest I miss a step—that my whole existence had become an exercise in anxiety and people-pleasing. No wonder I was miserable.

When I work with people who are admitted perfectionists, I try to articulate the link between perfectionism and fear of rejection. This often surprises them, and just as in our discussion of trauma, simply becoming aware of the origins of a problem begins to lessen its hold. Knowing this dynamic helps you own your stories, whether they're about perfectionism or anything else, and heal the connection to your inner creative self.

One tool to help overcome self-rejection and perfectionism is to write a poem.

The Power of Poetry

In my work with groups, I will almost always announce, at some point in the session, that it's time to write a poem.

And the group's reaction is almost always the same: a room full of horrified faces staring back at me.

"But I don't know how to write a poem," someone brave enough to object will say. Other heads start nodding, relieved that someone else said it out loud.

"I don't either," I reply with a shrug. "That's why it's so important. Poems come from your feelings, not reason, and we don't need to do it perfectly. We're here to revive your ability to feel, express, and create."

That's what we're doing in this book, too.

Before we begin, I want to remind you that it's not about writing a "good poem," or even anything that makes sense. The poem you create doesn't have to be in full sentences, and it definitely doesn't need to rhyme (many of my favorite poems do not). In short, I want you to drop any "rules" you have around poetry, as this is your chance to experiment with uncertainty, trust your inner voice, and practice choosing your words.

For this poem, I want you to choose an evocative image and write a poem based on all that the image stirs up inside you. You can choose this image in one of two ways: You could flip through any magazine or book, or scroll a website, until one grabs your attention. Another option is to go through some family photos (the older the better), and choose one that sparks something inside you. Whichever method you choose, try to move through the photos quickly until one gives you a little nudge. When it does, start writing immediately, jotting down any words that come up for you as a result of the image.

If you feel stuck, try writing words in any order that describe how you feel when you look at the image—the scene, the colors, or any other details. Consider the image through each of your five senses: sight, hearing, smell, touch, and taste. Allow yourself to be illogical, to not make any sense, to stretch and make connections.

In the following example, I had found an old manila envelope full of pictures from my childhood. I sat there on my living room floor and flipped through this stack of memories. One in particular stood out; it captured a moment with my younger brother. We were playing outside together and our faces were lit with excitement, innocence, and joy. So many feelings flooded over me, and a rapid succession of other memories—how my brother and I became adults, how we learned to turn away from that innocence and joy over time, how our lives grew heavier with the burdens of adulthood and the pressures of denying the child-like impulses that once came so naturally. I longed to recapture some of that old magic again. I sat there with tears in my eyes and then picked up my pen and notebook to write these words—fumbling at first, but then in a rush of feeling that brought with it the relief

of expressing things that had been kept inside for far
too long.

Hello
Remember me?
I love you
We started out together
You were amazing
We wondered at the world
rowdy playmates
sky painters
magic makers
remember Clothespins and peanut butter?
But I became stained
heavy
in trouble
Not safe.
They dressed us
We hated that.
You don't recognize me
But I didn't leave
I'm still wild,
I still want to play with you
To kiss you
To play hide-and-seek
To run and discover new paths.
So run away with me now
we can do it.
I'm still here
I'm waiting for you

Now it's your turn. Grab your journal and flip through some images until one strikes you. Just begin writing about it.

When you've written a string of words in whatever order they might appear, find a private place and read them aloud to yourself. This practice is not meant to push you into a public performance. I want you to feel and hear the expressions of your inner creative self in a safe space.

After you have experimented with this, ask yourself these questions: Do you feel exposed or afraid to craft an imperfect poem, even for your eyes only? Do you notice a twinge of relief or exhilaration as some part of you opens up? Please note in your journal whatever you are feeling—including irritation with me for suggesting such a thing or any resistance you may feel. All feelings are permitted here, and the real practice is to nourish a sense of safety and begin to send signals to your subconscious that you are good enough and worthy of being heard and seen and accepted.

Reclaiming Authorship of Your Story

When it comes to your own story, if you don't take time to understand how rejection and the other enemies of creativity have shaped it over time, it's like the story is writing you. The inner creative self takes a back seat, and the enemies of creativity take over. You may not even realize the impact these stories have, but they can lead to feeling uninspired, helpless, or hopeless in certain areas.

Becoming the author of your own life story allows you to reclaim all of the energy you've been unintentionally giving away. It enables you to stop being small and to step into the fullness of who you are. Being big doesn't mean you have to set up a billboard for everyone to see; it only means you're doing what you want to do, what brings you joy, instead of what you've been socialized to do or reacting to past trauma and rejection.

In looking at who we are in the stories we tell ourselves as well as those that are told to us, we also unlock powerful tools for our creative imagination. Rewriting our story can help us do things like share long-repressed emotions, bring imagination into reality, and point to deep truths about our experience that can't be expressed any other way. Stories are uniquely human, intrinsic to our makeup, and they can be a profound catalyst for change. No one can resist a good story—nor do they soon forget a good one—and I encourage you to write your story in a way that energizes you and brings you into your full potential.

As you do so, let's review the other two elements of story I mentioned at the beginning of the chapter, conflict and journey, and how these impact the overall narrative.

For many of us, conflicts—which would include things like unexpected problems, disappointments, challenges, etc.—are something we try to avoid at all costs. But the truth is that there is no great story without a conflict. Next to character, it's the most important thing.

Furthermore, resolving any conflict almost always requires undertaking some sort of journey or quest. Now, journeys and quests can be exciting, exhilarating, exhausting, or all of the above, depending on the story we tell ourselves about them. As we move toward being the author of our stories, consider the following questions in relation to conflict and journey:

1. What happens if the conflicts you face in life don't break or diminish you, but instead open you to new experiences and new possibilities for learning and growth?

2. What if the point of any given journey— whether it's a difficult day at work or a quest to change the world—is not to conquer, to fix, to save or be saved, but rather to feel, to learn, and to create?

Let's keep these two questions in mind as we rewrite our old, unhelpful stories. Of course, the first step is to recognize some of the unhelpful stories you've told yourself over the years, and one easy way to find them involves spotting two words I mentioned in a previous chapter: *should* and *shouldn't*. We've already discussed how they often signal the presence of an unhelpful story:

> I shouldn't have gotten divorced . . .
>
> I should have stayed in school . . .
>
> I should have gotten that job . . .
>
> I shouldn't have experienced . . .

After the words *should* or *shouldn't*, there typically follows a host of other details and self-judgments. In my own case, I recounted in the introduction how my life collapsed. Here is how I first told my story when my life was unraveling:

> This shouldn't be happening to me. I'm thirty-five years old and have done nothing but strive to do everything right up until now. Instead of getting rewarded, I've lost my business, credit, bank accounts, retirement—everything. I am afraid to show my face. I feel like a failure as a father, a husband, and a businessman.

From a writer's perspective, this kind of story is like a first draft, those early attempts that lay everything on the page, messy and unedited. Similarly, many of the stories we carry around with us are simply that: first drafts, unexamined and unrefined.

Most experienced writers will tell you that revising and rewriting are what lead to the best stories. Rewriting means you can consider alternative versions drawn from the same set of facts. I call this process *conscious storytelling*.

As I moved through the process of investigation and healing, I wrote a new story:

> At thirty-five years old, I received a very special gift. My outer life collapsed, and it led me to reconnect with my inner creative self. This journey, while painful, resulted in me finding a joy, peace, and sense of purpose like never before. Because of this, I am a better father, friend, and colleague, and in general a far more enjoyable person to be around. Today, I can honestly say that what I thought was the worst thing that ever happened turned out to be the best thing that ever happened.

While there are many ways you can rewrite a story, I'm going to ask you to consider a three-step revision process of acceptance, curiosity, and compassion, while keeping the two questions on page 99 in mind.

Acceptance

Because we so often tell stories that reject ourselves, our feelings, and our choices, the first step is to entertain the idea of accepting things just as they are. Start by naming the feelings involved, as we learned to do in previous chapters, and get as specific as possible. What does this story feel like in your body?

Next, see if you notice any patterns or similarities with stories from your past.

Finally, try a little radical acceptance: What if everything is okay just as it is? How would that change the story?

For example, I regret leaving school early, and it makes me feel inferior and terrified that I am a failure. My teachers often told me that I wouldn't amount to anything, so that's an old story for me—and in some ways I still believe them, despite being successful in a lot of ways. Can I accept these feelings and stop pushing them away? Can I trust that I'm enough and that learning new skills is available to me at any time, whether I'm in school or not?

Curiosity

Next, ask a few questions about each of the core elements of your story, including character, journey, and conflict. Ask yourself, *How can I revise this story to paint a more truthful picture? What is my role here? What other roles might I consider?*

For example, if you're looking at a divorce, you might want to consider the ways you and your partner relied on certain roles instead of showing up fully as yourselves. You might also want to begin and end your story in a different place. What if your trouble began long before there was any outward problem? Or what if your divorce was really a new beginning for you and your partner? This is not to minimize or change the pain involved, but rather to experiment with shifting your perspective on the situation.

Compassion

The next part of rewriting your story involves pulling back and remembering that you are the artist of your own life and this story is just one of many powerful creations you bring into the world and sustain on a daily basis. You can forgive yourself for telling or believing a story that isn't true for you. You're only human, after all.

For example, if you feel you should've gotten a job, you might ask, *What will help me remember that I am a work in progress?* You might also want to remind yourself that these kinds of disappointments are real and they really do hurt. Setbacks and difficulties are a normal part of life.

Sometimes your stories will want to stay planted as they are, and other times you'll find that the old beliefs and thought patterns about past events fall readily away. Often it is the passing of time that allows us to rewrite our narratives with acceptance, curiosity, and compassion.

No matter where you are with your own story, I want to stress the life-changing magic of radical self-acceptance. In my own experience, this has been the most helpful step in the process. The truth is that the most creative thing you will ever do is to become yourself.

Learning how to become yourself is at the heart of the creative cure. As you recover any lost desires and reorient yourself to your own true north, you'll often find that your passion for life grows. You'll notice a growing sense of purpose and fulfillment. Peacefulness and that essential state of joy become more often the norm rather than elusive moments that vanish so quickly. This is the promise of staying with the job of becoming yourself.

Exercise: Rewrite Your Story

This exercise is a two-parter. First, we'll try approaching an old story with a new perspective. Then, we'll see how adding an affirmation can help solidify your new story—one that more closely reflects your core feelings and beliefs.

Open your journal to the list of shoulds and shouldn'ts you made in chapter 3. Next, pick one that seems true for you right now as is, and write a paragraph or two filling in additional details of this story, just like I did on page 101.

Next, look at that story with the lens of acceptance, curiosity, and compassion. How could you creatively write a new one with the same set of facts? Remember that you are the main character here, so you're in total control of the narrative. Apply the two questions from earlier in the chapter as you do so:

1. What if the conflict you faced was for you to learn and grow?

2. What if the journey it required of you wasn't for a destination, but rather for you to experience, feel, and create?

None of this is meant to minimize the pain and suffering you faced, but rather to offer an opening to change your perspective. One way to play with rewriting this portion of your story is by flipping the word you originally used. For example, "I shouldn't have gotten divorced" becomes "I *should* have gotten a divorce." Now fill in the blanks on how this could be true. Is it possible this event allowed you to learn, grow, and become the person you are today?

Add an Affirmation

Finally, with a new story starting to take shape, try adding this affirmation practice:

Sit quietly on a couch, in a comfortable chair, or on the floor with your back supported. Play quiet music in your headphones or on your stereo, if you like. When you can breathe easily and feel yourself in your body, notice the floor beneath your feet and the ground or cushion that you are sitting on. Rest your back against the wall or the back of your chair.

Breathe in gently through your nose and repeat the following silently: *I am loved.* Hold it for a beat as you allow yourself to feel this truth. Release your breath slowly through your mouth, and feel all your anxiety, tension, and fear leave your body with it. Repeat silently: *I am safe.* Do this for a minute or two until you can feel the truth of these statements settle into your nervous system.

I often add a sequence. Breathe in: *I am seen.* Breathe out: *I am enough.*

No matter what's going on in the outside world, you can remind yourself of these inner truths: *I love myself. I am safe. I see myself. I am enough.*

You may also want to add some affirmations based on the work you've done with your story above. For example, you may have changed your story from "I shouldn't have gotten divorced," to "My divorce helped me to see that I can be a whole person all by myself, and I am stronger today because of that." With this in mind, consider making a short affirmation out of this to add to your affirmation meditation, perhaps "I am stronger today," or "I am whole."

Exercise: Detailed Instructions

This next exercise is one you can do by yourself or in a group setting, but to start I'd suggest doing it on your own. Grab your journal, and take a moment to think of a situation or problem that is causing you difficulty right now. This should be something that really stirs up big feelings or instigates familiar patterns of behavior.

Now imagine that you've been tasked with leaving detailed instructions for someone unfamiliar with your situation. The goal is that by following these instructions step-by-step, an imaginary person should feel just like you do. What are the ingredients of your current situation? How could it be recreated? You'll see that this begins to get fun—and funny—pretty quickly, and it can be a useful tool for turning a story on its head and reclaiming authorship of your desired outcomes. Here's an example:

Problem: I'm totally overwhelmed and miserable. My newly blended family is not blending at all, verging on all-out war between people who are supposed to love (or at least tolerate!) one another. If I were to guide another family step-by-step on the journey of getting to this place, here would be my detailed instructions:

First, make sure you have totally unreasonable expectations, such as kids should be kind and respectful at all times and adults should be levelheaded and unemotional always. This will hold every action, feeling, and thought to an unattainable standard, which is a proven path to misery.

Next, and this is really important, try *not* to communicate any expectations! Just keep them in your head and trust everyone to read each other's minds. This will keep everyone on edge.

Make sure no one has clearly defined space or time just for themselves.

Try to avoid laughing, being silly, dancing, or listening to music together. You might accidentally feel connected.

It's best if parents take on the role of referee for any dispute, large or small.

Everyone involved must deny their real feelings. Jealousy, anger, hope, and fear must be kept under wraps at all times.

Don't get outside and play on a daily basis, whatever you do!

It's best to bring up simmering resentments *only* when everyone involved is both hungry and tired.

Finally, make sure every person involved believes that we have to get this right, as soon as possible, and then be done with it. We're just trying to get to the end result, not waste time with a lifelong process of curiosity, generosity, and discovery about what it means to be a part of this unique family.

See how this works? By bringing creativity and humor to a situation, we can process some of our own unhelpful storytelling clearly without getting defensive or shutting down. We get some immediate ideas about things that might help our situation, everything from being silly and getting outside to making sure we're sharing our expectations.

Exercise: Failing Awesomely

For this exercise, I want you to pick one new endeavor that you think you might enjoy but that you know you will also do badly. Why will you probably do this new task badly? Because you've never done it before! Ideas for this might include drawing a self-portrait, designing and building a birdhouse, baking a complicated recipe from scratch, playing the harmonica, knitting a pair of socks, or ballroom dancing with your partner. Pick something you have never, ever tried before that you are guaranteed to screw up the first time. I mean it—instead of dreading the inevitable, you're going to embrace and look forward to your failure. After all, it's almost impossible to learn anything complex without making mistakes, and only by repeated failures can we begin to grasp a new skill.

For example, I have a friend who bakes bread. She's baked countless loaves over the years, and like many regular home bakers she rarely needs to consult a recipe anymore—she can whip up a golden loaf of rosemary bread whenever the mood strikes. Whole wheat, sourdough—she's tried it all. But her early attempts at bread baking were unmitigated disasters. Her very first loaf, in fact, has become something of a family legend; no one knew that you could make an actual brick out of wheat flour, but she managed it. When it hit the bottom of the trash can, she said, it sounded like she was throwing out a piece of furniture.

It's only natural to fail at a new project, and you might get frustrated, but try to make it a point to laugh a lot through the process. Give yourself positive "failing" pep talks, like "I'm going to make an unholy mess out of this right now!" or "This is going to be the most epic failure ever. They will write songs about how awful this is going to be." If you take yourself less seriously, you'll have more fun, and the more fun you have, the more you'll practice.

One day, you may find yourself failing at your own expectations by becoming a master harmonica player.

Exercise: Real-Life Kintsugi

The Japanese practice an art form known as *kintsugi,* or *kintsukuroi*, which means "golden repair." Artisans repair broken pottery pieces by using gold rather than adhesive to camouflage or hide the break. The resulting vessels are stronger and more beautiful than the originals. The cracks are not just repaired, they are celebrated, their very brokenness highlighted with precious metal.

For this exercise, think about a time when you felt broken, flawed, or imperfect and write a short account of the situation in your journal. Provide as much detail as you can, including how you felt about it at the time and how you feel about it now. If you still feel stabs of pain, self-loathing, or regret over what seems broken, ask yourself, *How can I repair this using the precious metal of my love, acceptance, and curiosity?*

Allow yourself to embrace your imperfections, knowing that what you create with the pieces becomes even stronger and more valuable. You can bring the same reverent creativity to your own healing and wholeness as the Japanese artisans do when they restore a broken vase with gold.

Exercise: Going Further with Poetry

Now, if you want to, go back to the initial poem you wrote earlier in the chapter and think about word choice, order, connectivity, etc., as this is a wonderful way to strengthen your creative storytelling.

Because the building blocks of stories are words, poetry is a great tool to help us feel, to become more mindful, of each one we use. Depending on how they are strung together, words can excite us, make us sad, fill us with inspiration, and help us express the range of emotions that color our human experience.

Because we are all storytellers, words are one of our most important creative tools, so paying attention to them and developing a new lexicon can pay big dividends toward developing our creativity. As we become more skilled, we can take great care when selecting the words that give life to our stories. The trick when "improving" any poem like this is to remember that you are only doing so for you. When I did this process to the poem I shared earlier, this was the result:

Remembering Life

Hello, says Life, Remember me?
We started out together here
When you were just
a bundle of amazement.
Remember how you saw the world
With nothing but wonder?
We were such rowdy playmates then.
We painted on the sky with clouds
And made magic out of
Clothespins and peanut butter.
Remember, can you, how I became stained and heavy
With trouble?
Not safe now. So much no.
They dressed me in painful clothes
And made you wear them, too.
You don't recognize me, do you?
But I've never abandoned you
Or lost my wild, happy desire
To show you
Play with you
Kiss you
Hide and seek down twisty paths
And always discover more.
Want to run away with me again?
Shall we elope without ever leaving
Because that's possible, you know.

I've never been anywhere but here
Waiting for you
To remember.

Six

Revitalizing Action Through Creative Practice

The biggest fear we have is not the fear of dying, but the fear to be alive, to be ourselves, to say what we feel, to ask for what we want, to say yes when we want to say yes, and no when we want to say no.
—don Miguel Ruiz

Each of us is bound by time, the one resource we can never renew. We are temporal creatures, here in our bodies on this planet for a relatively short interval. This is a basic, simple truth, and yet even writing or reading these words brings up a flash of heat in my face, a tightness in my chest. *Fear.* Faced with the reality of our limited life span, we fear death. In fearing death, we generate the even bigger fear that the powerful shaman and best-selling author don Miguel Ruiz speaks of in the quote above. We fear life. We fear living.

Paradoxically, when we find a way to embrace the inevitable limit of death, we release ourselves into the fullness of life. Many of the greatest artists and thinkers throughout history have been fascinated with death, keeping mementos such as skulls on their desks as daily reminders of something most of us would rather not consider. Why? Because death reminds us that we are alive and that our job as living people is to create, to be ourselves, to seek truth and share our insights with others . . . in short, *to live.*

Or, as poet Mary Oliver puts it, "Tell me, what is it you plan to do with your one wild and precious life?"

Remember how we defined creativity? Creativity is the process by which imagination becomes reality. Creativity brings something into the world that didn't exist before. I never feel more alive when I am in the midst of making something from nothing. When we create something, anything, we enact one of the most primal human impulses. The restoration of the relationship with our inner creative nature, therefore, provides the most expansive, inclusive path to living our one wild and precious life.

For me, this is a spiritual practice.

Most of us long for meaningful connection with our own understanding of spirituality, even if traditional religion doesn't appeal to us. The practice of creative expression in humans predates any formal religion. The incredible thirty-thousand-year-old Chauvet Cave paintings in France demonstrate an artistic skill that is comparable to anything the modern world has to offer. Human creativity is perhaps the oldest form of spiritual practice, and we've being doing it since long before we had words like *God, grace, or sin*.

Stepping back from ideas associated with religion, we can see how expressing the feelings and impulses of the creative self is spirituality in action—it's the literal weaving together of spirit and matter. The result is a greater sense of being alive, with reverence for life, and the ability to revel in the deep joy of living.

For me, spirituality and creativity describe the same thing: the way we celebrate the timeless, essential energy of life. Furthermore, since creativity as a spiritual practice doesn't dictate any particular beliefs or traditions, it can work in harmony with any other religious or spiritual customs you may also enjoy.

Through artistic practice, we connect to the greater energy and intelligence that powers the universe. This energy and intelligence, the source of life itself, offers the potential for astonishing and unexpected healing that we might otherwise never be able to access.

Here's a story to show what I mean. A friend works as a department head in a tech company, is the mother of three young children, and enjoys helping others in both her professional and personal life. She's intelligent, charismatic, and accomplished. One day, she felt a strong urge to start painting, though she didn't know why. She soon developed a love for coloring the canvas, and over the next few years she would paint on the weekends, though she never considered herself an artist.

One Saturday afternoon, something unexpected happened.

"I was sitting there moving the brush over the canvas and I forgot where I was," she began. "Then I went back to a time when I was very young, and I saw my mother brushing her hair after a round of chemotherapy. Clumps of it fell into the bathroom sink. I was overcome with sadness and helplessness, and I realized that I had kept these feelings locked down for so long. I kept painting through the memories, and I lost track of time—I sort of woke up a couple of hours later and this is what I had been painting."

She pointed to a large canvas, alive with light and color. In it, a hot-air balloon glowed with the light of the setting sun as it floated in a bank of dark clouds. I could feel the energy pulsing from the scene, though I would never have guessed the emotions that helped create it.

"I can't really explain it," my friend said. "It was like I worked through all of these complex old feelings as I painted. By the time I was done, I felt relief from a burden I didn't even realize I was carrying."

While my friend's experience is remarkable, it's not entirely unique. The field of professional art therapy has flourished in recent years as psychologists have discovered that art and body-centered therapies can reach hidden pain and foster healing and that creative practices can open the psyche in fascinating ways.

I have another friend who attends informal ecstatic dance sessions and tells me how moving her body to music restores her ability to feel joy and other emotions more fully. At times she finds herself in tears, as the movement and sound release old, rigid energy. "I go home feeling so much lighter every time," she says.

I believe we are meant to use creativity in all of life—not just in the arts. At the same time, returning to an art form, even in a simple practice, can be therapeutic, spiritual, and profoundly healing.

The process of inner work that we've done so far in this book is deeply creative and therefore deeply spiritual. It requires commitment and engagement of the whole being; it requires practice and imagination. Healing in this way takes time and in some instances continues for a lifetime. As I've said before, the relationship between creativity and healing is a kind of seesaw—we do one and then another, as healing opens creativity and creativity in turn feeds healing.

Any creative expression you pursue will reawaken your senses and help you remember the feelings of joy in creating. This heals your capacity for imagination and delight. Creative practices also reduce anxiety, provide a sense of accomplishment, and connect us to others and the environment around us. In short, they heal us in ways that nothing else can.

As adults, so many of us fall out of touch with our most playful, curious nature and abandon or mistrust our inner knowing, our accurate guidance system within. This leaves us to rely on direction from others, but sooner or later we realize that what's true for someone else may not be true for us. We wonder why we are unhappy, anxious, or unfulfilled.

Reverting back to our childhood traits can't save us, either. Children don't have the developmental capacity to handle the kind of rich, complex relationships with others that we seek as adults. They can't yet build deep self-knowledge or find meaning in the light and dark aspects of life. All of these are essential for lasting joy. You may even know a few adults who can't or won't embrace being a grown-up in a meaningful way, which can cause pain and trauma in its own way for them and their loved ones.

So if we can't return to childhood and we don't want to fall into a limited and deadly adulthood, how do we cultivate both openhearted expressiveness and the pursuit of unadulterated joy? Because of course there *is* something childlike about those people who have remained curious and passionate throughout their lives. As the great expressionist painter Matisse lost his eyesight late in life, he began to use large scissors to cut out sheets of colored paper. The results are astounding: a lifetime of artistic inquiry and visual exploration seems to have brought him back to the beginning, to the expression of a child. His simple, rough-cut figures come alive, open and playful, yet charged with the profound history of decades of creativity.

No wonder so many philosophers and spiritual sages throughout the ages have advocated the need to be childlike. Perhaps this is why we love artists so much, because they express their feelings with the openness of a child. They remember a way of seeing and knowing that most of us do not. They awaken our emotions, too, and inspire us to rediscover the delicious freedom of creativity. The author and poet Jason Reynolds describes freedom with a one-word synonym he created: *breathlaughter*. I'd like a daily dose of that, please.

What Is a Creative Practice?

When it comes to creativity, reading this book has hopefully reinforced why it's so important to nurture this healing force in our lives. Many of us are yearning for more imagination, deeper emotional connection, and expanded creative expression. So how do we accomplish this? Creative practice is the process of this work, the way it shows up and brings its many gifts to our daily lives.

We all know that a practice is something we do regularly with the goal of improving rather than completing or reaching an end goal. The word can also refer to something that's a habit or routine, and a creative practice offers us a tool to break out of old, unhelpful habits, refreshing our outlook on the world in new ways. Overall, practice is as important for masters of a field or art form as it is for novices. It's a journey, not a destination.

If you're just beginning a new creative practice, maybe for the first time since you were a child, I encourage you to be gentle with yourself. Remember that your efforts may feel awkward and uncomfortable at first. This is normal. Keep going for a little while when you try something new so that you have enough input to decide if this is something you want to develop into a regular creative practice.

Whether you're learning to bake bread or sing an aria, the magic of practice lies in two ingredients: mindset and commitment.

Fostering a Growth Mindset

You may have heard of a "growth mindset," defined by researcher Carol Dweck as the belief people have about themselves that their most basic abilities can be developed through dedication and hard work. A "fixed mindset," in contrast, maintains the belief that our skills and talents are basic qualities we can't really change, which leads us to spend our time displaying these qualities instead of cultivating them.

In my experience, the former is true, at least when it comes to creativity. I'm not alone in this, either, as countless other artists have said that their creativity continues to grow and develop throughout their whole lives.

That being said, one of the unhelpful ways in which mindset comes into play when it comes to creative practices is through comparison. If you are an aspiring writer, you may idolize James Baldwin, Delia Owens, or Liz Gilbert, for example. Singers may long to perform like Adele or Aretha Franklin. Allow your love of other artists to inspire you, of course, but be careful not to use the creative genius of others as a measuring stick of your own creativity. I believe that this is why the practice of creativity has felt elusive for many people. We compare ourselves to others and then reject our own work, not realizing we are rejecting ourselves and our pursuit of joy in the process.

The very definition of creativity means to produce something that is yours. I would go even further and say that engaging in your creative practice is synonymous with the practice of *you*. It is you practicing familiarity with, healing of, delight in, and expression of yourself as an art form. Comparison has no place in the particular art form of *being you*.

By bringing a growth mindset to the process, you open to the idea that the life you are living is a work in progress. I invite you to become your own best friend, your most loyal collaborator and creative partner in this endeavor. I invite you to make a lifelong commitment to your own creative practice.

Making a Commitment

What does commitment look like when it comes to creativity? At the most basic level, it means honoring a vow of self-love and self-valuing every day. This can be about dreaming, making plans, and following through. Go on adventures, take risks, try new things, and discover more about what really makes your heart pulse with joy. Part of your creative practice is the process of making time and space for all of the above with yourself. In any relationship, there will be moments filled with grieving or working through difficult things— but when you're committed to a creative partnership with yourself, you look for innovative solutions to come through these moments with new insight and strength on the other side.

Sometimes the inspiration to do so can feel elusive, especially if we're waiting around for it to strike in our artistic pursuits. Just as in a romantic partnership, we can commit to being there even on days we don't feel particularly inspired.

One way to foster commitment is to set ourselves up for success. Making our practice daily or at regular intervals keeps the door open for inspiration whenever it arrives. We can build creative habits through even the tiniest practices. Five minutes of daydreaming on purpose, deciding to make one sketch on a napkin or slip of paper every day, or putting together your daily outfit with conscious creativity—all of these count as practice! Plus, they tend to build on each other, leading to bigger artistic rewards.

When in doubt, go small and set the intention to do one thing a day. Repeating even the smallest creative actions builds up over time and pays dividends. I have a friend who has a note on her phone where she jots down a one-sentence plot idea for a story every day. Knowing she's going to do it every day takes the pressure off of having to generate profound ideas, or even good ones. Some of them are silly, but she knows that this moment of creativity will boost the rest of her day, connect her to her deeper insights, and sometimes even give her an idea she wants to flesh out further in her writing.

A New Way of Seeing

A fabric artist and quilter I follow has the most delightful Instagram feed of the everyday things she encounters. What makes her images captivating is the way she sees and shares them. A stick in murky water; a close-up of a leaf or a spoon. She is seeing the world in a way that would never occur to me, and I'm grateful for her exploration of subjects big and small through the particular lens of color, texture, and emotion that is all her own.

Creative practice offers us a new way of seeing. If you are learning an instrument, for example, your ears may become attuned to the strange sounds all around you—a lawn mower sustaining a steady note or the ditty that your washing machine plays at the end of a cycle. Artistic practice brings us home to our own singular way of experiencing the world around us. As we gain new perspectives, we access deeper understanding. We come into closer contact with our deepest, truest selves. This is part of the mechanism of healing through creative practice.

Joy as a Way of Moving Through the World

Many people think of a creative practice as time spent at the workbench pursuing their craft in a regular way. This is certainly part of a healthy creative practice, but we want to broaden the scope and meaning to include anything that helps us restore our connection to inner joy.

What if we began to see our whole lives as a kind of joyful practice? Every time we engage in creativity and the pursuit of joy, we're also alleviating or lessening feelings such as anxiety, stress, sadness, depression, and a host of other negative emotions and psychological clutter. Seen this way, joyful practice becomes a daily dose of good medicine.

One caveat as you develop this practice: Some people I've worked with tell me that they've struggled to establish creative practices because they see them as "things I should do." Notice the dreaded *should* there? There's no need to trade one form of socialization for another one, even if it's "better" or "more creative." I want to be clear: If painting isn't your thing, don't do it. If writing isn't your thing, don't do that, either. Through trial and error, you'll find a balance between committing to yourself and remaining flexible enough to release what's not working for you so that you may try new things as desired.

As we expand our sense of what belongs in your creative practice, here's a list of possibilities to inspire your thinking. As you read, pay attention to any hits of intuition or strong emotional responses of any kind. These might be pointing you to your next beloved creative endeavor!

- Baking

- Cooking

- Restoring old cars

- Rescuing or raising animals

- Gardening/farming

- Canning/preserving

- Landscape design

- Photography

- Making herbal teas/medicines

- Website design

- Interior decorating

- Space clearing/organizing

- Flower arranging

- Building personal altars

- Creating an invented language

- Architecture/urban planning

- Game design

- Carpentry

- Dancing

- Acting/directing

- Playing an instrument

- Singing

- Hairstyling, costume and makeup design

- Sewing and textile art

- Fashion design

- Jewelry making

- Knitting/crocheting

- Refinishing furniture

- Hand-spinning yarn

- Making your own *anything* from scratch (shoes, paper, candles, furniture, toothpaste, etc.)

- Growing a small business

- Community organizing/volunteering

You might also enlarge your notion of any of the traditional art forms. Visual arts can include watercolor/oil/acrylic painting, pencil/ink sketching, glassblowing, papier-mâché, wood carving, ceramics, collage, mixed media, paper cutting, cartooning/illustration, bookmaking, printmaking, mosaic, and so much more.

While we're at it, the field of creative writing goes far beyond the great American novel: book reviews, poetry, personal essays, blog posts, marketing copy, technical papers, recipes, prayers, song lyrics, speeches, rituals, comic books, plays, screenplays, personal correspondence, journal articles, family holiday letters, and more. You don't have to write a book to be a writer—though if that's your goal, definitely go for it!

We'll use this list for the first exercise at the end of this chapter to create the smallest possible building block of creative practice in one of these areas. This will get you on your way, but first I want to build awareness of the environment you create and nurture around your creative practice, and your creative community. This is your creative context, and it holds immense power to support and renew whatever art form you choose to pursue.

Creative Context

Once you find what makes your heart sing, engaging in it won't feel like strenuous gym workouts, a diet, or a restrictive budget. This is simply a path to greater creative joy. Now, sometimes we face boredom or resistance to any regular practice that we love, but that's often an invitation to get creative with our practice and to switch up our context.

For instance, I have a friend who is an accomplished writer and has a regular practice of writing four or five days a week. He loves what he does, and if he goes too long between writing sessions, he starts to feel like something is missing: the skies of his life begin to look dark, the colors of his relationships seem to dull, and a sense of general melancholy sets in. Because he has learned this about himself, he writes regularly.

Yet—and this is partly because it's also his profession—there are some days when he just doesn't want to write. His solution has been to change his writing location, his creative context, and that most often does the trick. So while he has a wonderful writing room, he will sometimes take his show on the road, and you can find him writing on his laptop in parks, coffee shops, or parked in his car. Anytime you're feeling stuck with a creative practice you know you love, ask yourself what you can do to get creative with your creativity.

What if you apply the notion of creative context to your physical space? Does your home or office inspire creativity? Is there anything in it that shuts you down or leads you down an unhelpful path of comparison, shame, or numbing habits? Creative context can also apply to the time you make for creativity in your life. Whatever it is, begin to think of your creative practice as it relates to your whole existence, not just as a one-off thing you sometimes do. Think of building a beloved habitat for your inner creative self.

A vital, organic, sustainable creative practice can range from small moments of slowing down to engage with our emotional selves, through simple art exercises, to daylong excursions designed to delight and reinvigorate your inner artist and muse. Julia Cameron calls these artist dates, and there's an exercise to build these in the following pages. We can also expand our creative practice with powerful artistic rituals born out of the unique expression of emotion, intuition, and storytelling that is our own life. We will explore a few of these in the exercises section.

Creative Community

In most schools of Buddhism, there is a concept called sangha, which is one of the three jewels of Buddhism, the other two being the historical Buddha and the dharma, or teachings. *Sangha* is translated as "community of practitioners," and I find it interesting that it is considered equally important as the other two jewels for progress on the spiritual path. Beloved author, teacher, and Buddhist monk Thích Nhất Hạnh says, "When you allow yourself to be in a sangha the way a drop of water allows itself to be in a river, the energy of the sangha can penetrate into you, and transformation and healing will become possible."

Prior to learning about sangha, I guess I had the idea that being a Buddhist monk meant sitting alone all day in meditation.

Then I was reminded of a widespread myth of the solitary creative—the artist laboring in (possibly tortured) isolation to create a masterpiece. It's common to think of the artists we revere working away in walled gardens or lonely garrets, rarely venturing into the company of others. The reality is quite different. If you ever look at the the works of the impressionist painters, many of them depict scenes with the likes of Gauguin, Van Gogh, Monet, or Seurat hanging out together over leisurely meals in cafés on Paris's Right Bank. Hemingway enjoyed the company of F. Scott Fitzgerald, Yeats, James Joyce, Gertrude Stein, and Max Perkins, among many others. Even Henry David Thoreau, famous for his writings on solitude, spent time with Emerson, the Alcotts, Nathaniel Hawthorne, and others in the Concord neighborhood not far from Walden Pond.

So while it's true in both Buddhism and creativity that regular times of solitude are essential, the truth is that we learn and benefit from being with each other, too. Humans are social creatures by nature. While the degree to which we need interaction may change from person to person, there is a part of us all that is at its best when we are sharing ourselves with others.

For these reasons, I prescribe regular connection with others in our creative practice, as doing so can help our heart sing in ways that solitude cannot. I also know that it's essential that the creative sangha one chooses be marked by positive regard, acceptance, and genuine enthusiasm for each other rather than competition or criticism. Otherwise those things will stifle the spirit of real community, as they can discourage the kind of vulnerability and trust that genuine connection requires.

Many aspiring creatives form or join groups in the hopes of gaining encouragement and improving their skills. And you will likely find that the people you invite into your world need you just as much as you need them.

Julia Cameron coined the term *creative clusters*. She encourages her students to post a note on a local bookstore or library bulletin board with something like, "Writers wanted for local creative support—please contact (name) at (email address or phone number) if interested."

There are many ways to form such groups now—online using social media or neighborhood connection websites or Meetup systems. In my experience, a gathering of even just two or three, whether in-person or virtual, to share in the creative journey together is transformational. I'll share some guidelines for starting your own creativity group in the exercises that follow.

Exercise: Tiny Habits

Inspired by the work of habits expert B. J. Fogg, this exercise couldn't be simpler. The purpose of it is to get yourself going in a new or renewed creative practice.

First, grab your journal and answer this question:

What creative practice would bring more joy into your life?

If you're not sure, settle in with the list in this chapter and slowly read through the suggestions. Allow your body to be relaxed and open. Breathe. Notice any negative stories that come up through socialization. For example, maybe it's something like, "I can't work on old cars; I don't have the money for that kind of hobby," or "I'd like to learn to dance, but I don't have time to take classes." Set those aside for the moment, and let yourself dream.

Once you've come up with one or two options, write a list of possible answers to this question:

What is the smallest habit that could bring me toward this practice?

When I say small, I mean *really* small—something that seems almost ridiculous to commit to. (Fogg famously advocates the habit of flossing one tooth, with the idea that once you've started flossing, you're likely to keep going with all your teeth.) If we're thinking of dancing, a small habit might be to look up one salsa move and commit to practicing it once a day. That's it. Don't overcommit—just keep thinking about that one little move.

The magic is in the repetition. I think you'll find that the joy you feel when you get started with a daily practice will undoubtedly inspire you to do a little more than you had planned on. That's how the creative practice will start to become habit. I suggest you try it and see what happens.

Exercise: Walking to Boost Creativity

We know walking is good for our physical bodies, but in 2014 a team of researchers at Stanford found that walking helped increase creative inspiration, sometimes in a big way. In fact, one experiment even found that walking produced *twice* as many creative responses to the researcher's prompts compared to sitting, and the creativity sparked by walking continued even after sitting back down after a walk.

This exercise is simple. Take a walk! If you want, start with a "tiny habit" of going to the end of your block and back. (Once you're outside, you can always walk farther than you'd planned.)

Here are a few ways to boost walking as a creative habit:

- Before you sit down to write, paint, or work on a project, take a ten- to twenty-minute walk in your neighborhood.

- Make an imaginative game out of your walk. Give people or things you see secret names, and greet them as you pass by—out loud or in your mind. Tell yourself a story about any one thing you see with a beginning, middle, and end.

- Leave devices behind. For a creativity walk, focus on what's happening around you, and the sensations or emotions you're feeling inside as well. What does it all feel, smell, taste, look, and sound like?

- Allow yourself to be bored, do nothing, and zone out.

- Note that the Stanford researchers were surprised to learn that we get the same creativity boost walking outside or inside, in a hallway, on a treadmill, or down a forest path.

- Change up your walk by trying a new route, playing with pace, or throwing in a few different steps or dance breaks as you go. There's a wonderful set of videos online of a woman who put up signs in front of her home designating it a "silly walk zone" and then taped the delightful antics of walkers young and old as they played along.

Exercise: Enliven Your Creative Context

In order to keep inspiration flowing and your creative practice alive and sustainable, you'll want to take a look at strengthening your creative context.

Just as it's easier to eat well when your kitchen is stocked with healthy, delicious foods you love, building a creative practice will benefit from putting some forethought and planning into what will best support your efforts and eliminating or minimizing anything that will make it harder or less pleasurable.

If we think of creativity as a ritual or spiritual practice, this can help us honor the time and space we dedicate to connecting with our inner creative self. For me, treating this as sacred time and space opens up new possibilities for presence, joy, and healing in my whole life—not only special creative moments.

Here are some common elements you might want to consider as you play with finding your creative context. Take some time to journal about what these mean to you, and change whatever you want to build up your creative environment.

Space. Whether you have a whole room for your creative practice or just a corner, what makes your space feel most creatively friendly to you? For some, it's a place they're not afraid to make a mess, while for others cleanliness and decluttering is essential. Does your space have a speaker for music? Or a special playlist in noise-canceling headphones? Incense or scented candles? Can you make the most of the lighting by swapping out bulbs or adding fairy lights? How can you play with color in ways that draw you into the space? What books and artwork inspire you? Think of the textures: living plants, polished wood, a square of marble on a desk, or rugs underfoot.

Time. Spend a few minutes thinking about how time can be your creative partner. I love using a timer for quick, contained bursts of writing, for example—whether it's five minutes or an hour. Also consider what time of day suits your creative practice best. Everyone is different, and you might want to experiment. Finally, part of building a strong creative process is creating as much of a boundary around time as you can. Yes, creativity will be your friend and partner always, but setting aside some protective time for artist dates or a particular creative practice is essential. Honor this time as sacred and let those around you know that you won't be available. Even if you can only carve out fifteen or twenty minutes, do it.

Ritual. Time and again, I'm struck by the creative rituals of writers and artists. Casual or elaborate, earnest or playful, these rituals transform ordinary moments into focused, sacred time that builds meaning and honors the inner creative self.

In my own case, every day before I begin writing in my journal, I take off my shoes and physically walk around my couch and coffee table three times. I'm creating a sacred circle when I do this, and it's deeply personal and restorative. The circle ritual reminds me that this is my physical and emotional place to try anything without fear of rejection or criticism.

I encourage you to experiment with marking the beginning and end of your creative time with a ritual of some kind. Here are a few ideas you might try:

- Lighting and extinguishing candles

- Reciting poems or prayers, or singing a song or chant you particularly love

- Shaking a rattle or beating a drum

- Asking your muse to meet you in the space

- Doing some stretches or taking a number of deep cleansing breaths

- Setting out and cleaning up your materials with intention

- Washing your hands and face in scented water

- Putting on a piece of special jewelry or clothing

- Putting your hands over your heart and saying the words *thank you*

Simple ritual actions like these show your conscious and unconscious mind that you are making time and space for something important. Remember to stay open and flexible, changing things as needed, and bringing your creative context wherever you go.

Exercise: Forming Your Own Creativity Group

Setting aside some alone time for creative projects is wonderful and fulfilling on many levels, but there's also something to be gained by sharing your endeavors with a group. You can trade ideas, help each other problem-solve, and just make each other accountable for putting in the time on something that's important to each of you. I'm in a small creative group myself, and our guidelines are simple:

1. Show up.

2. Be honest.

3. Speak from the heart.

4. Share experience rather than give advice.

As our group has become closer, we've added a promise to hold everything that is said in the circle in strict confidence, never disclosing outside of the group or referring to anything shared without that member's permission. We have also agreed to air any discomfort or grievances with each other directly in a process called housecleaning. This fosters an atmosphere of trust and freedom unlike anything I've ever experienced before.

Over time, I've found that I can share both my art and my heart with the group without fearing the response. I've also learned to listen in a whole new way. This experience in my creative group has changed how I show up in every other relationship in my life, as I've brought those same principles into my interactions with others. This is an example of what can happen when we are invited into emotional trust and intimacy with others, and even life-toughened men are capable of this in the most remarkable way.

I'm sharing this with you because I recommend using these simple principles to guide you as you seek creative community. With very little formal structure you can invite others to join you and offer each other open hearts, nonjudgmental listening, and encouragement in the process of unfolding your creative dreams.

What would you do in a group like this?

The first thing would be to either share your art with each other or create art together. You may also want to do some of the exercises in this book, or the ones found in *The Artist's Way* by Julia Cameron.

You can get together and spend a few minutes sharing about your lives and what you're working on, then turn on music and write for an hour in silence together. My friend Lauren Sapala formed large groups like this in Seattle and San Francisco around the idea of silent writing. While she works mostly with writers, you can use this time for any kind of creative expression.

For example, you might start with the practices of self-discovery and self-acceptance I have offered in this book, journal together quietly for twenty or thirty minutes, and spend the next half hour or hour sharing your discoveries. You might meditate together and experience the mysterious connection that can develop in a group setting. If you use the principles of honesty, compassion, confidentiality, and no unsolicited advice, you are likely to leave each time of connection feeling seen, heard, and inspired to keep growing.

Please remember fun, too. Nothing makes a group cohesive like genuine laughter. There's something that happens when we're honest about ourselves with trusted others. It generates laughter as we admit our quirks, flaws, and the ridiculous moments of being alive. Take walks together, sit together, go on adventures together, share meals, and mostly share yourself.

There's big medicine in dissolving the shame, distrust, fear, and isolation that many feel every day by forming a creative sangha where we are safe to be seen and heard—where each person is invited to feel that they are enough just as they are. That we belong, here, with these people, as ourselves.

Seven

The Creative Formula—
Magic in Real Life

To bring anything into your life,
imagine that it's already there.
—Richard Bach

When I began the work of reconnecting to my inner artist and reshaping my life on my terms around a whole new set of priorities, I was flying in the dark. As so often happens with any kind of big life change, I knew I had to let go of unhelpful beliefs and patterns, but I didn't yet understand how I would ever be able to live without them. I could feel—literally sense in my body—the urge to strike out into new territory and make new discoveries. This urge for freedom from my past traumas and socialization inspired and motivated me to commit to a future I couldn't yet grasp. At the same time, it was as though an invisible force were pulling me back toward old habits and ways of thinking. Why? Even if my existing habits were making me miserable, at least I understood them—they felt familiar and comfortable to me in some way.

I didn't have a road map to guide me through what would be a bumpy and sometimes painful journey. I yearned for something solid, some way to know that whatever challenges I faced, they were bringing me closer to the life I deeply desired and deserved, the life I was beginning to feel I was responsible for building. Only years later, in large part through working with others, did I start to see certain patterns emerging. I have few regrets in life, partly because I believe that failure is my best teacher, but I do wish I'd been able to access the wisdom of those patterns earlier, something I now call the creative formula.

The good news is that I can offer the magic of this formula to you, so that you can put it to use right away in your own journey. We've already been learning about most of the elements of the creative formula throughout this book, so now let's take a look at how they all fit together:

Imagination + Feelings/Intuition + Story = Action/Results

I would argue that any single creative action—by which I mean anything that brings something into the world that didn't exist before—functions so through this formula.

Any result you want to achieve, or action you want to take, happens by way imagination, feelings, and story. This is true at all levels, from the cup of coffee you make for yourself and savor in the morning, to fulfilling a lifetime goal of climbing Mt. Everest. Think that sounds crazy? I mean it.

Coffee

Imagination: Lying in bed, I can taste and feel the warmth and kick of that cup of coffee.

+

Feelings/Intuition: Desire, excitement

+

Story: If I get out of bed and go into the chilly kitchen, this will yield the reward.

=

Actions/Result: Grinding beans, brewing a pot, and sitting down to enjoy

Mt. Everest

Imagination: It's been a lifelong dream to make it to the peak of Everest.

+

Feelings/Intuition: Exhilaration, fear, courage, determination

+

Story: By putting in the effort and going step-by-step, I can achieve this goal.

=

Actions/Result: Researching, training, allocating resources, pushing to the top

Any creative act can be broken down into this formula. Furthermore, the creative formula is at play *whether or not you are conscious of it*.

We've already examined the ways in which we use the creative formula to unconsciously create scenarios we *don't* want: Your imagination paints fearful scenarios. Your body feels the emotions associated with those scenarios. You tell yourself and others an unhelpful and untrue story. You take actions that are now based on fear rather than the pursuit of joy. This is a recipe for unhappiness, one we've all followed to the letter time and again.

Whether you're manifesting what you'd like to do this weekend or how you'd like to be of service in your community over the course of your lifetime, your biggest ally is your inner creative self. Throughout this book, we've looked at ways to open and heal the connection to this part of yourself, freeing you to express your deepest desires and truths. By engaging in this process, you align the creative formula with what you truly desire. You bring consciousness to a process that for most people remains mysterious. The formula needs to be used properly so it can work to your advantage in any creative endeavor, large or small.

Why a Formula?

So many of us think of creativity as an inexplicable lightning-bolt moment of achievement. If someone is talented or lucky, wonderful things *just happen*. It can certainly feel like that when we're on the outside of someone else's creative process looking in. We only see the end result. This is why I've distilled the creative formula over the years and called it something that sounds more like chemistry than art. By taking it apart and putting it back together in this way, we demystify creativity. Paradoxically, many artists and thinkers speak of their greatest creativity coming in moments of limitation or strict rules. I've watched countless people discover this as they use the creative formula—believe me, the formula aspect of this won't shut you down; it will actually expand the possibilities of your creativity.

There are two main reasons we need this formula. First, it's a tool for dreaming our wildest, most inspired dreams—the kind of dreams that come from our truest selves. Not only does the formula inspire this kind of dreaming, it helps us in formulating a plan to make our dreams real in the world. It gives us concrete steps for what can otherwise feel like an amorphous, touch and go, luck of the draw process. Second, it can serve us when we're stuck. Very often we don't (or can't) see the ways in which we're sabotaging our own dreams and plans. The formula provides a checklist, a way to take apart the elements of the creative process and examine them one by one. In this way, we can find out what's working and what's not, and we can see what's missing in the execution of our deepest desires.

The Creative Formula of This Book

This might seem a little meta, but let's look at the magic of the creative formula in terms of the results you are holding in your hands right now (or reading on a screen or listening to me read you): this book.

When I started writing this book, my feelings of overwhelm and intimidation threatened to derail my genuine desire to complete it. I knew I was somehow blocking the creative formula, layering in negative self-talk and imagining unwanted outcomes. Since I could identify my own resistance and self-sabotage, I took my feelings of overwhelm into my daily journaling practice.

Each day, I challenged myself to get quiet and allow my inner self to imagine and describe a scene in which this book was already completed. I envisioned the faces and lives of people I wanted to serve with the ideas and strategies in these pages. I imagined how it touched people's hearts, opened their synapses to new ways of knowing, and instilled confidence as readers all over the world reconnected with their inner creative selves and healed their lives.

I needed to keep repeating this step of *imagination*, and each day the images I was creating in my journal grew stronger and more detailed. Sometimes, my fears took over, and my imagination would paint vague scenes of failure. I practiced acknowledging these fears while not giving them ownership over my creative process. Over the course of a few weeks, I could see and feel the finished book even though the contents weren't yet completed. Perhaps more importantly, I was building an imaginary picture of readers who found this or that section particularly exciting, challenging, or inspiring. I could hear their questions, which led me to write passages to address their worry or confusion so that they could keep going deeper into the work. I felt the warmth and support of working with my mentors, editors, and publisher, all of us circling around the important themes in the book so that they could be expressed in the clearest way possible.

These images brought me into contact with the next part of the equation: *feelings*.

Whenever I allowed my imagination to follow its habitual tendency to create a scene of failure or risk, my feelings were heavy and filled with anxiety. By turning my inner attention to the version of a possible reality that I desired, the feelings followed along. I became filled with enthusiasm, curiosity, joy, and gratitude.

When my thoughts and feelings were aligned on what I wanted to create, I would often get nudges from my *intuition* that appeared as thoughts in my mind's eye: "include a section on this"; "research the effects of that." By listening to them, I was cooperating with my muse. The book began to take shape, page by page.

Can you see how consciously enacting this formula began to change the outcome?

By using my imagination, creating the feelings that I wanted, and listening to my intuition, I fueled the *story* I told myself about the book. This part is key, as the words we use to describe our progress toward a desire or our capacity to reach a goal can either multiply the effects of our imagination and feelings in a positive way or reinforce more of what we don't want. The choice is ours. It's a simple shift, but sometimes it takes a lot of courage and focus since we're so used to telling and hearing negative stories.

Our inner creative self also has a very strong bullshit meter. In other words, we can't make ourselves believe a story that doesn't feel true for us. We can, however, change our perspective so that we can focus on a story that holds a bigger truth than the one told by our worst fears and most minimizing lens.

In my case, this meant honoring the story I was telling myself about my worries that I wouldn't be able to communicate clearly or finish on time. I began to write a few sentences in my journal to describe this negative story. And then I would consciously pull back and tell a different, equally true, story. I began to refer to the process in positive terms:

> I know that worries are part of the process of making something I'm proud of, but the bigger story here is that I am grateful for the opportunity and responsibility to share what I've learned. So much of the writing of any book is about the thinking, reading, and preparation—all of which I've been doing for years. In that sense, this book is coming along so well . . . I can really feel it taking shape.

When people would ask me about it, I found myself reinforcing my imagined outcome and feelings with words like, "I'm discovering so much as I go. It's really coming together day by day," rather than expressing vague despair or apologizing for my work. Hafiz once wrote, "The words you speak become the house you live in." Remembering this helped me begin to create a different "house," or result, by paying attention to the story I was telling myself every day.

When we figure out the most helpful story that feels true for us, we really begin to build momentum. Each of the pieces of the creative formula can now come together and flow into the actions and results we are after. Yes, writing this book did require me to sit down for hours and do the work, just as anything you wish to accomplish will in its way. Because I had done the work on the other parts of the equation—on the imagination, feelings, and story—I was able to focus those hours of action in alignment with my deepest desires. I was able to enter a flow state, as my inner creative self felt free to express. Whenever I got stuck or felt out of alignment, I could return to my journal and dig into my imaginative vision for the project, how I was feeling about it, and the story I was telling myself.

Everyday Magic

For me, the creative formula is a kind of everyday magic. To be clear, I don't see magic as trickery or something fanciful, but rather the application of a higher order of universal law that can seem to supersede the rules of the lower orders. Just as in America, where federal laws overrule state or local legislation, magic is simply what happens when you employ natural laws of order that transcend usual existence. When we think in terms of magic, we open ourselves up to the possibilities of the unknown. The most elemental forces of nature, from gravity to the interplay of pieces of genetic code in any living thing, feel like magic to me. When we have the courage to break from our conditioned patterns of thought and behavior, we allow these expansive forces of magic into our lives.

We can do this in simple, everyday ways by using our imagination, listening to our feelings and intuition, and changing our story. We might also be surprised by a bit of out-of-the-blue magic in the form of a miracle. I like to define a miracle as something good that happens that didn't seem possible given the circumstances.

By this definition, some of my favorite miracles include the following:

- Falling in love

- The birth of a child

- Healing a past trauma

- A tree growing out of a rocky cliff

Let me invite you into this kind of real magic.

Think about something you would love to create, something that's always been blocked by things seemingly beyond your control. Wouldn't it be a miracle by my definition if you could use higher principles to create that thing in your life?

Your inner creative self already knows these laws, deep down. It was formed as a result of them. You got here because of a combination of imagination, desire, story, and actions. You are the result of the creative formula in action.

Because of this, it is your birthright to use the principles of your natural self and create a life and everything in it that reflects who you really are.

Let me also remind you that the actions you need to take—the *how*—will show up as you focus your attention, desire, and will using this formula. The skills and resources you need, people to help, and strategies to accomplish your endeavors really do begin to appear as needed. Furthermore, the actions you need to take are often far less difficult or daunting than you think. When your imagination, emotion, and story are aligned with your inner creative self, the necessary actions may often surprise you by being simple and quite doable. I don't know exactly how to explain this, but when you activate the creative formula and train it on something you desire, you activate a field of synchronicity and serendipity. Things begin appearing to support your progress and make it reality. As Goethe said, "Be bold and mighty forces will come to your aid."

Using the Creative Formula for Dreaming and Planning

The first way to put the creative formula to work is to use it to create a desired result—a big dream, an impossible miracle, or something much simpler. People often say to me, "Well, this sounds great—but how do I use it, you know, in the real world? I'm not writing books or starting companies or inventing things yet, but I do have things I'd like to change in my life."

Your creative nature wants to express itself in every area of your life, but you may want to pick one or two small, practical things that you would love to change. Think of some area in which creating a different result would bring you joy and satisfaction. What if you transformed your basement or your backyard into a place you'd love to relax in? You can use the creative formula right now, beginning with something at home. It's a wonderful place to start.

Remember the magic question that puts you in the proper mental state to use your imagination: *What would I love to create?* This sets your subconscious mind on a track, searching for the answers to this powerful query. Whatever you answer will land on the right-hand side of the formula: the actions and results. Then you can begin to build up the other side, the imagination, emotion, and story. Let's practice it now.

Open your journal to a new page. Start at the top with the words,

I am so joyful and grateful now that . . .

Take a moment to land on just one thing that you'd love to change—a new result you'd like to create. Picture how you would love it to be, appear, and feel. Describe it in the present tense.

For example:

I am so joyful and grateful now that I'm sitting in my backyard on a warm Saturday morning. I see that new stone wall over there with flowers spilling over it. I love how the breeze feels on my face, and that it surrounds me with the smells of my lush garden. I can hear birds in the branches and the cool stone of the bench I'm sitting on. I feel so relaxed here and safe. This place is my sanctuary, and I come here to rejuvenate and find peaceful solace.

By doing this in your own words, you're unlocking the door of your imagination. Your attention begins to create a vivid image of what you would love to have happen.

Do this for a couple of journal sessions, and as you write, you can change perspective by moving your imagined self around in time and space. What will your garden feel like in the winter? How will the tiny creatures in your backyard feel? As you go, take stock of and list whatever emotions you're feeling as you imagine your end result. Pay attention to any intuitive "hits" that bring new information on ways to create the space you want or questions to pursue that may lead to new discoveries. Get curious about the story that brought you to this desire. Acknowledge and bring forward any negative version of the story. Is there a bigger truth you can dig into there? Rewrite your story in a more positive light.

Once you've developed a movie in your imagination and really felt into the emotions of the end result in your mind, you can take a look around at the scene in current reality. Returning to the garden project, you may find that when you look out your back door, things feel depressingly far from what you imagined.

Don't get discouraged—this is a good thing!

This creative tension is what can bring clarity about the distance between two points: your desired result and current reality. Creative tension is a lot like what happens when you pick up a bow, fit an arrow, and pull back the string. Even without a bow, you can close your eyes and imagine doing this. As you do, can you feel how your muscles tighten and the pressure builds?

When it comes to anything you desire to create, when you allow yourself to be clear about the distance between the two points, you will feel tension. This can be uncomfortable, but it signals that you are engaged in the act of creation. That's why I say it's a good thing. It indicates that you are on a creative path and that your mind and body are engaged in the process.

Sometimes people encounter this tension and interpret it as stressful or "too much," and this leads them to abandon their project. When this happens, take some quiet time to listen to your inner self and learn whether this particular desire is coming from your true joy. If it is, the tension powers you forward, despite the fact that it's not comfortable at first. If not, then you are free to let go of an idea that may be a result of others' expectations.

Once you have allowed the image and feelings to develop clearly and reinforced them with a positive story, you can ease up a little and let your creative self offer the next step forward in the direction of your desired result. Intuition can come into play here, and I have also found that the first step frequently seems ridiculously small. Remember the tiny habits we talked about earlier in the book? The same rule applies here. Locate the smallest possible move forward. Let's say you want to work toward a new career, but the idea feels overwhelming. After you've put together the first parts of the creative formula equation, you may find that the next obvious action is to check job listings online or make an appointment with a résumé expert. I find that by honoring each step of the creative formula, next actions seem to flow quite naturally.

Problem-Solving Using the Creative Formula

I believe that getting stuck can be one of our greatest gifts. Not that it feels great, but we all know that when we attempt any creative endeavor that's worth our time, we're bound to encounter challenges and conflicts. I have a dear friend who's developed a wonderful habit in response to when something goes wrong or otherwise unexpected in her plans. She immediately stops what she is doing and says to herself with excitement, "Plot twist!"

By using the tools in this book to open up your creativity, imagination, and joy, you too are building your capacity to respond to difficulties in innovative ways. When you get stuck, look at each portion of the creative formula and see what's missing. Often by tweaking one thing, you unlock a treasure trove of inspiration and action.

- Have you taken time to truly imagine your creative outcome, tapping into each of your senses in the process?

- Are you owning up to your emotions and letting them flow?

- Are you open to any intuitive nudges about what to do here?

- What about your story?

I have a friend who had a crystal clear goal of making a ceramic arts space where she could do her own work as well as teach others the craft. She felt certain that she was using the creative formula in the best possible way, and yet she wasn't seeing results and kept hitting roadblock after roadblock. She spent months doing the hard work of envisioning, feeling into the emotional possibilities, and examining and writing her story. Then one morning as she wrote in her journal, she made a discovery: part of her story was about her own idea of what it meant to be independent. She realized that she had been attached to the idea that she had to accomplish this goal on her own for it to be worthwhile. As it turns out, this story wasn't really true for her; it was a holdover from her childhood. So she spent some time dreaming up what a collaboration might look like. Within a week, an opportunity dropped into her lap to join a collective arts space. Much of the hard work she thought was ahead of her evaporated, and she arrived at her dream more easily and comfortably than she ever thought would be possible.

Overall, the key to making the formula work for you rather than against you is to use it consciously and regularly. I spend a little time each day on my journal and meditation practices using this formula with everything: issues with my children, how I would love to grow financially, my next creative project.

I encourage you to start small and simple, so that you activate the positive feedback loop that comes with using a new skill to accomplish something meaningful. The more you practice this, the more it becomes reflexive in your everyday life. You might find yourself pausing right before a potentially difficult meeting to ask, *What would I love to create in this situation?* When that happens more often, you know that you are on your way to creative living and expression in every area.

Exercise: Troubleshoot a Dream

Is there anything you once longed to do, or that brought you joy, but you let go because it was too difficult or something got in your way?

Maybe you gave up playing the piano, wrote the first half of a novel, or gave up on exploring new cuisines in meal planning and cooking at home. Or is there a creative dream that you've been working on that feels stuck or out of balance? Maybe you've been grinding on actions that seem to be taking you nowhere, partly because you've been neglecting the imagination, story, and emotion parts of your project. Alternatively, you might be blocked at the imagination stage: you can see your result and feel it, but the story about your own worthiness and how you might realize your dreams remains a messy first draft.

Today, pick up one of these long-lost creative pursuits and do a little refresher on each of the aspects of the creative formula. If it helps, imagine that it's a new endeavor. How would you approach it from your current reality? What's been missing from the creative formula that you can refresh or think about in a new way?

Go through the process described in this chapter for dreaming and planning, and then arrive at your next smallest action. See if you can reinvigorate a dream that got stuck along the way with the magic of the creative formula.

Exercise: Personal Discovery Assessment

Now that we've covered the creative formula in detail, take the look at the personal discovery assessment I've included as an appendix in this book. As you will see, this tool invites you to look at the major areas of your life and find out where you are in relation to each of them. With this info in hand, you can decide where you may want to try applying the creative formula. I have found that combining the daily Creative Self Journaling practice with this assessment—and with some form of meditative or relaxation practice—allows you to gain the clarity you need to begin making all of the creative choices toward a reality that will bring you always-growing joy in the art that your life is meant to be.

Eight

The Work of a Lifetime

A genius is the one most like himself.
—Thelonious Monk

Opening up to self-discovery and self-acceptance can be frightening. As Carl Jung said, "The most terrifying thing is to accept oneself completely." Echoing this sentiment, many of my clients have shared with me their deep fear of knowing what's hidden inside them. They worry that entering into this work will expose something secretly rotten, dirty, or fatally flawed.

In my experience, the exact opposite is true. Rather than finding out how broken we are, self-discovery reveals more about the true self, which is always perfect in its original, unique design. Often, the things we are most worried about exposing end up being the most powerful parts of our personality once we decide to accept and cherish them.

This is the work of a lifetime. The more you learn about yourself, the more you will find that you are intrinsically acceptable. You can release old patterns that no longer work for you. In the resulting atmosphere of unconditional positive regard for who you are, you are free to grow into more of your potential. This is the essence of the word *transformation*: changing form as you explore what is possible and true. This is the work of a creative life, and this is its greatest joy.

Lao Tzu explained the surprising benefits of self-discovery and self-acceptance this way: "Because one believes in oneself, one doesn't try to convince others. Because one is content with oneself, one doesn't need others' approval. Because one accepts oneself, the whole world accepts him or her." This is a direct reversal of the way many of us were taught to seek approval and acceptance from the outside world. Mysteriously, when we enact Lao Tzu's words, we often begin to receive more outside acceptance than we ever have before. Anyone who is living their truth with joy becomes magnetic.

In the ongoing seesaw of self-discovery and creativity, when we become more comfortable in our own skin and operate in alignment with our natural design, we discover more creative capacity in all areas of our lives.

There's a saying that often motivates people when they set out to build a life they love: "If you do what you love, you will never work a day in your life." While I agree with the sentiment, I also know that on some days—perhaps many days at first—creating a life you love can be hard work. Transforming your life brings challenges. Excavating your sense of purpose can be difficult, buried as it usually is beneath so many layers of conditioning and fear. You are worth it. Your healing is worth it. And the world needs the creative spark that only you hold.

The Gift of Joy

When I was very young, my father was a violin maker. One of my earliest memories takes me back to my five-year-old self, crossing the backyard in the early evening to his shop. I opened the door, and he turned from what he was working on and motioned me over. I stood at his elbow for a while, and then he picked me up and sat me down next to him on the workbench.

He was bent over a solid chunk of maple, cutting away the wood in long curls with one of his sharp tools. I watched his face, intent and focused as he worked. He had sawdust and sweat on his forehead. Once, his hand slipped and the blade sliced into the ball of his thumb. I rarely heard him swear, but in this moment he did. He shook his hand, stuck his thumb in his mouth, then took it out and covered the wound with a rag. Later, he bandaged it and went back to his work.

Violin making is a hard, exacting craft. Not only must one carve slabs of flame maple and spruce into the shape of a violin, but the shape must be precisely right if the violin is to make music. It is art and science combined. My father labored for many hours over each instrument.

What's equally amazing to me is that no one taught him how to do this. He searched through manuals and experimented for years as he perfected his craft. I now play one of the violins that I watched him make when I was a child. He was a complex, frustrating man in many ways, but he showed me what it meant to seek joy in excellence. Though he was rarely outwardly joyful or lighthearted, he nevertheless taught me an important lesson about the true nature of joy.

When he handed me one of his violins as a special gift after I became an adult, I could see in his eyes that this work was, in the words of poet Kahlil Gibran, his "love made visible." While we never could see eye to eye in many ways, he taught me by example that joy is different from ease. Joy is even different than happiness.

Joy arises from the expression of our true nature. Joy is like the natural aquifers that lie far below the surface of the earth. Sometimes a geyser or spring gushes easily at the surface, but often one must dig down into the dirt, exerting tremendous effort to draw the water upward.

Just like that underground water, joy is always there, even during times of sorrow, confusion, or depression.

You may remember that we started the first chapter with the idea that joy is our guide. Now we end where we began, in search of real joy. My promise to you then, and now, is that if you can redefine creativity for yourself and see yourself as an artist, you can revive joy in your life. I am doing this work today, and I will keep doing it tomorrow. I'm so thrilled you are joining me.

The Creative Cure

The system of socialization that we all created together over many thousands of years demands fear and compliance in exchange for a small payment of certainty. To make this system work, we have to shut off many vital parts of ourselves so that we can fall in line with order and conformity. We were born into this world, and those who brought us up trained us to behave for survival, just as they had been trained.

It's not anyone's fault, and we aren't victims. But you and I have a choice: Do we want a life of survival, or do we want to reclaim our inner creative nature? Will we step up and let go of the illusion of safety and approval so that we can embrace what is alive and calling us forward?

As you know from reading this book, the creative cure lies within you. Your joy and truth have been there all along. The medicine is in the answers that you find as you live into the question, *What do I want to create in my life?*

As you do this, you will find that joy lives in the process of doing, including solving problems that will inevitably arise along the way as you're creating something new. This joy—this payoff for doing the hard work of self-discovery, self-acceptance, and expressing your creative nature—has been there all along, waiting to sustain you.

By following along and doing the exercises in this book, you are accepting the challenge and joining the ranks of creative humans. As you live your life in this way, you make the world better for yourself and for your family, friends, coworkers, and anyone who enters your sphere of influence. You release the anger, heal the wounds, and banish the lies that have kept us locked in generational patterns of pain for so long.

Creating the life you desire may not be easy at first, but living it out will call you into the most creative, artful version of yourself that you can imagine. This question is your guide, your mentor, and your healer: *Where is my greatest joy?* When you live out the answers in your everyday life, gestating your joy, and giving birth to a new reality for yourself, you become the creative cure.

As you heal, love, accept, and grow into yourself, you increase your experience of the artful, intuitive life; you reclaim optimism; you restore your energy to accomplish what matters to you; and you enjoy a renewed sense of radical aliveness. You might feel darkness and pain more deeply, but it will have more meaning. You are safe, resourceful, and strong. These are the qualities of the inner creative self. If this promise comes true even in part, isn't it worthwhile to take the cure?

In closing, I'll repeat the words of the brilliant philosopher and activist Howard Thurman: "Don't ask what the world needs—ask what makes you come alive, and go do it. Because what the world needs is more people who have come alive." As we come to the end of this book together, I am so aware of the challenges we face in this world. These are not new things. They are as old as the human species, but there are more of us on the planet than at any time in recorded history. On one side, this can appear to be a grim situation, filled with unsolvable problems. Our minds are quick to tell stories of despair—or we are tempted to believe that we must expend all of our energy in hard work or joyless causes toward "saving the world." It's easy to believe that becoming creatively alive and joyful is frivolous or even selfish.

You know what I would love? I would love you to join me in seeing a deeply connected world—one in which the health and balance of every person is medicine and helps to heal the whole. I would love it if you can help me ask the powerful creative question, "What if . . . ?" "What if my life can heal and flourish? What if this is me doing my part toward everything else the world needs to also heal and flourish?" And, "What if I am enough, just as I am, living in my joy that grows stronger, deeper, and richer day by day as I become more of who I really am?"

What if, you know?

Afterword

You know how every once in a while
you do something
and the little voice inside says,
"There. That's it.
That's why you're here . . ."
and you get a warm glow in your heart
because you know it's true?
Do more of that.

This is your creative birthright,
the joyful art of self-discovery.
In the face of those formidable enemies
of creativity,
the socialization,
the trauma,
the rejection,
you heal.
Restoring imagination,
renewing intuition and emotion,
reclaiming the power of story,

revitalizing action
through creative practice.
Look at you . . .
you are an alchemist,
the elements of love, of curiosity, of play.
This is magic in real life.
This is the path of creative joy.

Acknowledgments

When I released the book previous to this one, I wrote the acknowledgments and pretended that no one ever reads this section, which left me free to say almost anything. To my surprise, that became one of the most commented-on sections and made me wish that I had included more people—and that I had spoken of them more colorfully, even.

Writing a book isn't the solitary process that many people imagine it to be. Writing this one taught me about that more profoundly than ever before. It seems to be a great exercise in trust. Trust that the shape of something good is forming within; trust that the many half-starts and piles of what might turn out to be nothing but word-garbage can become worth sharing with others; and trust in the creativity and vision of a team to bring it into being.

My publisher, Randy Davila, brought his tremendous skill for seeing structure in the thickets of words and ideas to this book, and I'm grateful for our friendship and all of the ways he invested (including so much patience!) in this project. As he worked on the manuscript with the editing team, many more pages were cut than made it into the manicured work that you've just read. This material becomes fodder for essays and other things that I will share in the future, so you can thank him for that, too. He's more than just my publisher, though. I've known and worked with Randy in various ways for over a decade, and he has been a mentor, friend, and guide—I know that I've become more of who I really am through our connection. I'm also grateful to the team he has assembled and led at Hierophant Publishing through the process of making this book a reality: editors, cover designers, manuscript designers, and those about whom I don't even know but who played a crucial part. Thanks to them and to you, Randy.

It must be obvious how much I have learned from Julia Cameron. My father handed me his copy of *The Artist's Way* in 2009 as I was going through the more terrifying part of self-discovery that followed leaving behind my previous identity. "I think this might help, but please bring it back to me someday when you're done with it," he said. He died the following year without knowing what a rich part of my life *The Artist's Way* had already become. Julia's work became a lifeline as I learned to use her tools for my own creative recovery. That's why when I had the chance to meet her several years ago, I was starstruck at first. When she made it clear that she would like to develop an actual friendship, I knew that something very special was underway. She is a deeply real human and one of the purest artists I've ever met: sensitive, committed to her craft, and unbending about staying focused on her soul work. Our friendship is one of my life's treasures. Thank you for that, Julia—also, thank you for helping me even before our friendship began and now with this finished book to repay my father for giving me that first introduction to your work. I feel that this has completed something very important, and I'm grateful.

My mother had prominent places in the original manuscript drafts that didn't fit the finished work, but she shared with me her love of beauty, books, words, imagination, hunger for self-discovery, and . . . life—using, among many other things, her wicked sense of humor and an astonishing vocabulary in several languages. Her honesty and courage as a human to overcome incredible difficulties and recreate herself over and over again have inspired me to just keep going no matter what. In her third act, she decided to go back to college and earn her master's degree in psychology, which she achieved with highest honors and is now a counselor. In that process, she came to me often, needing to talk about what she was learning about childhood trauma. We healed together as we shared tears over past experiences and what we were discovering about ourselves, each other, and the world. This has led to a new era in our relationship that is marked by freedom, trust, and much deeper love. I wish that every child of a mother had the gift of doing this sacred work with theirs as I have with mine. Thank you, Mother. You are evidence that real-life miracles are possible.

SARK—which is the acronym for a marvelous human named Susan Ariel Rainbow Kennedy—entered my life as a friend and guide after this book was already written, but she needs a place here because she did important work with me in healing and dissolving limiting beliefs about what is possible as a creative. Thank you for showing up exactly on time and in the perfectly magical way you did, SARK. It's obvious why millions of people around the world credit you with opening their hearts to what's possible. You've done it for me, too.

Is this the part where the music starts playing and the person over on the other side of the stage motions that it's time to wrap up the "Thank you" speech?

My list of thank-yous is as long as life itself. My children, brothers and sisters, friends, those who have attended my courses, clients, readers . . . everyone has played a part in helping me do the work and play of becoming more of who I am—which includes writing this book. I'm grateful to all of you. As I often say or write, "Thank you for being here." You are all constant reminders that becoming oneself is the ultimate creative endeavor. And yes, I do mean you.

Appendix

In keeping with the self-discovery work of the early chapters of this book, this assessment can help provide clarity about what you've created so far in your life and serve as a basis to develop a new plan for those areas that aren't currently fulfilling.

Before you begin, I want to ask you not to judge yourself or your answers as you fill this assessment out. There are no right or wrong answers here. Rather, use this assessment as a tool to discover where you want to bring more joy into your life.

You are the architect and artist of your life. No one else can create it for you! The goal of this assessment is to help you notice any areas that need to be repainted, resculpted, or rewritten.

Complete each section as quickly as possible. No need to overthink it. Allowing your feelings and intuition to come forward uninhibited will provide surprising insight and clarity.

Please relax as you feel into your answers. These responses are for your eyes only and designed to foster curiosity rather than judgment. You are likely to think of other questions or areas of your life that aren't listed here. Write them down! This is your creativity at work.

Part One: Work and Finances

Work is love made visible. —Kahlil Gibran

Most of us spend a large percentage of our time at work and paying bills, saving for the future, etc. When our finances are out of whack, it makes it difficult to prioritize space and time for creativity—saving money seems paramount, and financial uncertainty can make it hard to dream big. Working through the questions in this section will help you clarify your current financial position, prioritize your career intentions, make time for your art, and infuse your efforts with a sense of meaning and purpose.

Please rate the following statements on a scale of 1 to 10 (1 = Strongly Disagree and 10 = Strongly Agree).

1. My job challenges and inspires me. I look forward to going to work. _____

2. The ways I earn a living nourish me rather than exhaust me. _____

3. My income is adequate to support my life-style comfortably. _____

4. My debt load is manageable, and I have a plan to be debt-free. _____

5. I have savings and emergency funds.

_____

6. I feel peaceful about my finances and my financial future. _____

Notes

Use the space below like a mini-journal. How do you feel about your answers? Do any action items for changing the areas you aren't happy with come to mind? List them here if so.

_____

_____

_____

_____

_____

_____

_____

_____

_____

_____

_____

_____

_____

_____

_____

_____

_____

_____

_____

_____

_____

Part Two: Community

You really won't know where your home is until you meet your own kind and realize you're both playing the same game. —Shannon L. Alder

Your community includes your life partner, children, natal family, friends, and extended connections. Do your relationships feed your life or diminish your energy? Clarity in this area will help you make choices about where to improve, make changes, and set boundaries.

Please rate the following statements on a scale of 1 to 10 (1 = Strongly Disagree and 10 = Strongly Agree).

1. My romantic or life partner relationship is loving, supportive, and characterized by evolving intimacy and friendship.

———————

2. I do my part to have strong, loving connections with my family. I communicate with them often, and we share important life events together. _____

3. I have a circle of close friends. We support each other and share in healthy ways.

_____

4. I have good connections with a wider circle of acquaintances and groups of people who share my interests. _____

5. I think of others' needs and make an effort to be helpful when possible. _____

Notes

Use the space below like a mini-journal. How do you feel about your answers? Do any action items for changing the areas you aren't happy with come to mind? List them here if so.

_____

_____

_____

_____

_____

_____

_____

_____

Part Three: Wellness

Don't move the way fear makes you move. Move the way love makes you move. Move the way joy makes you move. —Osho

Do you have a strong, healthy foundation to support the life you want to live? Use this section to spot places where you need to improve your self-care and activities that will nourish and fulfill you.

Please rate the following statements on a scale of 1 to 10 (1 = Strongly Disagree and 10 = Strongly Agree).

1. I like my body—how it looks, feels, and moves. _____

2. I am physically active on a regular basis and/or have an exercise routine that is healthy and sustainable. _____

3. I take time to read, learn, and otherwise feed my mind. _____

4. I have a meaningful, consistent spiritual or mindfulness practice. _____

5. I love being creative in my own way, and I engage in making my art regularly.

    _____

6. I have hobbies that are interesting and enriching, and I engage in them regularly.

    _____

Notes

Use the space below like a mini-journal. How do you feel about your answers? Do any action items for changing the areas you aren't happy with come to mind? List them here if so.

_____

_____

_____

_____

_____

_____

_____

_____

_____

_____

_____

_____

_____

_____

_____

_____

_____

_____

_____

_____

Part Four: Environment

*Home is a state of mind. A place of communion and uncon-
ditional love. It is where, when you cross its threshold, you
finally feel at peace.* —Dennis Lehane

Like your physical body that houses your mind and
spirit, your home and style of living can provide joy
and comfort, or it can be a place that doesn't feel good
and drains you.

Please rate the following statements on a scale of 1
to 10 (1 = Strongly Disagree and 10 = Strongly Agree).

1. I enjoy the region I live in. It's where I want to live. _____

2. My house and furnishings reflect who I am and how I want to live. _____

3. I find inspiration in my space and neighborhood. _____

4. I enjoy traditions and meaningful events in my home with friends and family.

   _____

5. My home is a place of respite, connection, and peace. _____

Notes

Use the space below like a mini-journal. How do you feel about your answers? Do any action items for changing the areas you aren't happy with come to mind? List them here if so.

_____

_____

_____

_____

_____

_____

_____

_____

_____

_____

_____

_____

_____

_____

_____

_____

_____

_____

_____

_____

_____

Part Five: Inner Self

A self is not something static, tied up in a pretty parcel and handed to the child, finished and complete. A self is always becoming. —Madeleine L'Engle

Your inner self, or your inner essence, is the true you at the deepest level. Until we become comfortable in our own skin, it is very difficult to create lasting change in the other areas of life. A strong sense of self becomes your intuitive guide and helps you move in the direction of your heart's desire in every other area.

Please rate the following statements on a scale of 1 to 10 (1 = Strongly Disagree and 10 = Strongly Agree).

1. I am comfortable in my own skin; I like who I am. _____

2. I often judge myself, get down on myself, or berate myself internally. _____

3. I am my own best friend. _____

4. I am clear about my values, but also open to evolving and exploring ideas outside of my accustomed mindset. _____

5. My values guide my actions at home and work, even when no one else is watching.

   _____

Notes

Use the space below like a mini-journal. How do you feel about your answers? Do any action items for changing the areas you aren't happy with come to mind? List them here if so.

_____

_____

_____

_____

_____

_____

_____

_____

_____

_____

The Creative Cure

Conclusion

Take a short break, then read over your responses. Notice which areas feel light, good, and healthy and which areas feel heavy, painful, or toxic.

As you do this, try to stay relaxed. If you haven't taken stock of these things in some time, you may be surprised by the number of items that come into sharp and unpleasant clarity. You don't need to fix or address all these things at once. This is important!

This exercise is not meant to be a pretext to large, sudden life changes. You may need time, guidance, or professional help to transition to a life that more closely matches your true self, in a way that is loving to you and to those around you, while not sacrificing your honest desires.

Continuing Exploration: Listening to Yourself

Set aside a time to quickly make a list of every current "mess" you can think of in your life. Nothing is too small or insignificant: a shoe with broken laces, the overdue oil change, an imbalanced friendship, an unsatisfying job or relationship, and beyond. This is a process of allowing space to pay close attention to your needs, irritations, preferences, and what you have been tolerating.

You can write these things out in long sentences and stories, or in a simple bulleted list style. List everything that does, could, or should bother you in your life—especially those you pretend are "no big deal" or shouldn't really be a problem. Be specific and thorough.

You'll notice that this exercise of listening to yourself frees up much-needed energetic space. Your creative nature is primed to fill the open space and help you transform each of these areas in ways that will delight you and inspire further growth.

About the Author

Jacob Nordby is a writer living in Boise, Idaho. You might find him on a trail in the nearby foothills or typing away in the quietest corner of a coffee shop downtown. Learn more about his other books, speaking, online courses, and creative guidance sessions by visiting www.jacobnordby.com.

books that inspire your body, mind, and spirit

Hierophant Publishing
8301 Broadway, Suite 219
San Antonio, TX 78209
888-800-4240

www.hierophantpublishing.com